Families, Children, and the Development of Dysfunction

Developmental Clinical Psychology and Psychiatry Series

Series Editor: Alan E. Kazdin, Yale University

Recent volumes in this series . . .

Families, Children, and the Development of Dysfunction

Mark R. Dadds

Volume 32.
Developmental Clinical Psychology and Psychiatry

SAGE Publications
International Educational and Professional Publisher
Thousand Oaks   London   New Delhi

For information address:

 SAGE Publications, Inc.
2455 Teller Road
Thousand Oaks, California 91320

SAGE Publications Ltd.
6 Bonhill Street
London EC2A 4PU
United Kingdom

SAGE Publications India Pvt. Ltd.
M-32 Market
Greater Kailash I
New Delhi 110 048 India

Printed in the United States of America

Library of Congress Cataloging-in-Publication Data

Dadds, Mark R.
Families, children, and the development of dysfunction / Mark R. Dadds
     p. cm. — (Developmental clinical psychology and psychiatry ;
  v. 32)
    Includes bibliographical references and index.
    ISBN 0-8039-5191-4 (cl.) — ISBN 0-8039-5192-2 (pbk.)
    1. Mentally ill children—Family relationships. 2. Problem
families—Mental health. 3. Parental influences. I. Title.
II. Series.
RJ507.P35D33   1995
618.92'89—dc20   94-28879

95 96 97 98 99 10 9 8 7 6 5 4 3 2 1

Sage Production Editor: Tricia K. Bennett

To Paula

CONTENTS

SERIES EDITOR'S INTRODUCTION

Interest in child development and adjustment is by no means new. Yet only recently has the study of children benefited from advances in both clinical and scientific research. Advances in the social and biological sciences, the emergence of disciplines and subdisciplines that focus exclusively on childhood and adolescence, and greater appreciation of the impact of such influences as the family, peers, and school have helped accelerate research on developmental psychopathology. Apart from interest in the study of child development and adjustment for its own sake, the need to address clinical problems of adulthood naturally draws one to investigate precursors in childhood and adolescence.

Within a relatively brief period, the study of psychopathology among children and adolescents has proliferated considerably. Several different professional journals, annual book series, and handbooks devoted entirely to the study of children and adolescents and their adjustment document the proliferation of work in the field. Nevertheless, there is a paucity of resource material that presents information in an authoritative, systematic, and disseminable fashion. There is a need within the field to convey the latest developments and to represent different disciplines, approaches, and conceptual views on the topics of childhood and adolescent adjustment and maladjustment.

The Sage series **Developmental Clinical Psychology and Psychiatry** is designed to uniquely serve several needs of the field. The series encompasses individual monographs prepared by experts in the fields of clinical child psychology, child psychiatry, child development, and related disciplines. The primary focus here is on *developmental psychopathology*, which refers broadly to the diagnosis, assessment, treatment, and prevention of problems that arise in the period from infancy through adolescence. A working assumption of the series is that understanding, identifying, and treating problems of youth must draw on multiple disciplines and diverse views within a given discipline.

The task for individual contributors is to present the latest theory and research on various topics including specific types of dysfunction, diagnostic and treatment approaches, and special problem areas that affect adjustment. Core topics within clinical work are addressed by the series. Authors are asked to bridge potential theory, research, and clinical practice and to outline the current status and future directions. The goals of the series and the tasks presented to individual contributors are demanding. We have been extremely fortunate in recruiting leaders in the fields who have been able to translate their recognized scholarship and expertise into highly readable works on contemporary topics.

In the present book, Dr. Mark Dadds examines the many ways in which the family plays a central role in mental health and dysfunction of the child. The book is rich in coverage, beginning with historical underpinnings of the study of the family in relation to child development and dysfunction. Issues related to identification, assessment, and treatment of child dysfunction in relation to family processes are detailed. Alternative conceptual views of the family, critical features of family life and how they operate, and findings regarding the role of the family are presented and carefully evaluated. Specific types of dysfunction (e.g., depression, conduct problems, anxiety) are presented to convey the manifold ways in which family influences can operate. The ways in which the family has been studied, encompassing alternative measurement domains and methods as well as research designs, are also covered and evaluated. Overall, the book provides a remarkable integration of substantive findings, critical analysis, and directions for future work.

—Alan E. Kazdin, Ph.D.

PREFACE

A young man is shot in a gang fight. A youth is arrested and the talking heads of the media tell us of his unsavory history: an unstable home life followed by school failure and repeated arrests for minor juvenile crimes. His family are shown mourning and pleading for understanding for the troubles they had raising him: "We did our best, he wasn't a bad boy." Three young children are found locked in an apartment, hungry, and depressed. The young mother has thrown herself from the top of the building after a day in which the chores of caring for her young children finally overwhelmed her. An angry 13-year-old girl is brought into a hospital by her parents. They complain that she no longer eats at mealtimes, instead following a rigid routine of exercise, dietary pill abuse, and occasional binge eating episodes followed by self-induced vomiting. The interviewing clinician is impressed by the way the girl's problem seems to be a part of a very troubled family marked by marital problems, poor communication, and power struggles.

Stories such as these are now common in the media of almost any large city on earth and a stunned world watches, unsure of what to do or, indeed, if anything can be done. Of course, most examples of human behavior problems are not as dramatic as those above. Still, enormous resources are spent on programs to fight drug abuse, family violence, teenage pregnancy, juvenile crime, school truancy, graffiti, and a host of other problems. Increasingly, commentators point to the changing role of the family in modern society as being partly to blame.

It is a natural assumption, a part of our folklore, that children's mental health is largely a result of their upbringing. The idea of the "dysfunctional family" as the main cause of human behavioral and emotional problems now exists in epidemic proportions. However, most of us can also think of examples of children who were unable to cope with the demands of everyday life who came from wonderful families. Are there critical family characteristics that are reliably predictive of childhood dysfunction? Can these characteristics be modified by family therapy?

This book focuses on four aspects of the relationship between families and child dysfunction. The first is the historical. What approach have behavioral scientists taken in the past regarding distressed children and their families? The second is the methodological. That is, what sort of science can actually permit us to draw clear conclusions about the influence of the family on children? Third, we will examine the extent to which this sort of evidence is available. What part does the family play in the genesis of mental health versus mental disorder? How much variance in mental health outcomes is attributable to various aspects of the family life? What are the critical aspects of family life, if any, that affect the child's psychosocial development? Finally, we will examine the clinical data and implications of the above. Can these critical family factors be modified?

Throughout, the emphasis is on *experiential* or *learning* influences of the family on the child. It is not within the scope of this book to cover the possible genetic paths through which psychological dysfunction may be transmitted in families. Data on the heritability of traits that may predispose children to emotional and behavioral dysfunction are constantly being updated. For some problems, such as obsessive compulsive disorder and multiple tic disorder, the evidence is strong for a genetically transmitted component; for other disorders, the evidence is lacking (Rutter et al., 1990). In this book, genetic influences will only be considered to the extent that the genetic influence has clearly been shown to have an impact upon learning experiences within the family that affect the child's adjustment. Those interested in genetic aspects of child psychopathology are referred to the Rutter et al. (1990) article for a good starting point.

Thanks to Matthew Sanders, my long-standing colleague and friend, who easily could have been an author of this book because of the influential role he has played in the development of my ideas. Similarly, thanks to my wife, friend, and colleague, Paula Barrett, for her inspiration, support, and personification of family therapy as empowerment of children and parents. Thanks to the many children and parents who have worked with me in clinical and research contexts over the last decade. Finally, thanks to the University of Queensland, and in particular the Psychology Department and the Behaviour Research and Therapy Centre, for the years of support.

1

INTRODUCTION

THE CASE OF PETA

Let us begin by considering an example of a childhood disorder as a way of setting the scene for this book. This case was assessed and treated by the author and has been previously described in more detail in Schwartz's (1992) *Cases in Abnormal Psychology.*

Every day for the last 6 months, the same drama unfolded. Upon being picked up at school, Peta, 8 years old, and her mother would make the short walk from the school gate to the car. Peta would become more and more anxious, peppering her mother with questions about whether her books, pencils, pens, and even her teacher would be safe during her absence. Peta was terrified that the world of her school classroom would somehow disappear during the night and that, on her return the next day, she would find everything gone. Despite her mother's attempts to calm her, Peta would become increasingly anxious and upset until, agitated and in tears, she would run back to the classroom to check if her desk, work materials, and teacher were still there. On bad days, the returns to check on her things could last for an hour or more.

Similar problems were emerging in the home. Peta had begun checking the daily garbage to make sure that none of her possessions was being thrown out. If her parents tried to stop this checking, which sometimes was repeated over and over as if she were terrified she had missed something, she would become hysterical and act aggressively toward her parents. Similarly, Peta was developing a habit of checking on her parents, especially her mother, to make sure that she was "still there," that she had not disappeared or left the home. Clearly, Peta had little faith that her world would remain intact. She felt compelled to check on the important things in her life, lest her anxiety that they disappear overwhelm her. However, her checking offered only a temporary relief and the anxiety would return quickly, compelling her to check and check again, never fully satisfied that she had not missed something.

Both maternal and paternal sides of the family had a clear history of psychopathology. An uncle and the maternal grandmother had a history of schizophrenia, as well as depression and compulsive checking behavior, respectively. The deceased maternal grandfather had a history of alcohol abuse and, according to Peta's mother Liza, had physically and sexually abused Liza throughout her childhood. Peta's father, David, reported that his father also abused alcohol and was rarely living in the family home due to a predilection for aimless wandering. During his times in the home, he was violent toward his wife and the children. David's son by his first marriage and Peta's stepbrother, Thomas, had a history of conduct and learning problems that had resulted in school failure and dismissal as well as repeated trouble with the police.

David and Liza reported that their marriage had been unstable and that, at times in the past, David had been physically violent. David presented as a generally happy and talkative fellow with a history of osteoarthritis and heart disease, the latter having required a period of hospitalization approximately 4 years prior to referral. Peta was frightened by her father's heart problems, aware of the possibility that they could lead to further hospitalization and even death. Liza presented as mildly anxious and with a history of recurrent depression. She had very poor self-esteem and this was constantly reinforced by the power structure of the family in which David made the decisions and afforded her little respect. Over the last 8 years, she had almost totally immersed herself in the care and upbringing of Peta as a way of undoing the painful memories of her own childhood and to prove to herself that she could achieve something worthwhile. To David, Peta's problems were simply a matter of lack of discipline from his wife. To Liza, the problem was far more ominous. Aware that both her family and her husband's family had a history of mental illness, she was scared that Peta was showing the first signs of schizophrenia.

During middle childhood, Peta suffered a number of losses. First, her older brother and sister both moved out of the family home and out of state. Next, her grandfather died, another close intimate of Peta's. Her parents reported that Peta's grandmother began teasing Peta about the possibility that others in the family could die soon as well. Next, at the time of transition into the fourth grade, Peta's teacher had become ill and virtually disappeared from Peta's life. The parents reported that Peta would cry at night about not seeing this teacher, expressing constant fears that the teacher was either dead or dying. Soon after, Peta's mother then returned to work as a cafeteria assistant in a job that demanded working late at night. Peta would follow her mother out to her car, visibly distressed and asking her not to go. Over these 2 years, Peta had also suffered the loss of three pet cats from car accidents.

Against this backdrop of loss in Peta's life, there appears to be a particular event that triggered the actual checking behavior. Her performance of daily chores was suffering and, in particular, she was refusing to clean up her room. One weekend, her father, frustrated at the state of her room and tired of the constant battles to get her to clean it up, took matters into his own hands and removed everything from her room that he did not consider necessary. Peta had become hysterical during the cleaning, but she was unable to stop him. The parents reported that her checking of the garbage began the next day and the checking of her school possessions began the next week. These problems had persisted at a reasonably stable level since that time.

In terms of contemporary diagnostic categories, Peta's problem is an example of obsessive compulsive disorder, in which the sufferer becomes trapped in a world of anxiety and repetitive behavior. Obsessed with an anxiety-provoking thought, the sufferer compulsively engages in repetitive, ritualized behavior in an unsuccessful attempt to cope with the anxiety. In this example, Peta's obsessive thoughts concerned the possibility that various aspects of her life would suddenly disappear. These frequent, intrusive thoughts caused her considerable anxiety—anxiety that she had no understanding of or skills for dealing with. Consequently, she would compulsively check the environment in vain attempts to relieve her worry.

Peta's problems could be seen as a result of genetic vulnerability mixed with environmental stress. Both sides of her family have a history of schizophrenia, substance abuse, and general conflict. Her mother's side also may have had a history of obsessive compulsive problems. Notwithstanding this, it is important to consider Peta's overall adjustment in relation to its interpersonal context. When one considers the nature of the stress Peta had experienced, the form of her problem seems understandable. That is, the obsessions and compulsions represented her attempts to find stability and consistency in an unpredictable environment. In terms of the specific nature of Peta's obsessive thoughts and compulsions, it is useful to focus on the interpersonal and intrapersonal processes that may be *maintaining* the problem. These factors may be very different than the factors that were associated with the onset of the disorder. For example, a therapist might consider that the loss of significant others was the original reason that Peta began obsessing and ritualizing. Logically then, that therapist might prescribe a treatment that focuses on helping Peta to grieve appropriately and thus resolve her feelings about the losses. Family and social learning therapists may agree that the losses were associated with the onset of the disorder and that grief work may be useful. However, there is no reason to hold that the loss continues to be the reason that the behavior persists. On the contrary, it is likely that the problem behavior, once established, is now being maintained by environmental, interpersonal factors.

When a person displays unusual or inappropriate behavior, their "normal" behavior becomes less salient. Peta's parents were worried about her checking behavior and were constantly on the lookout for it. When it would occur, they would immediately attend to her and employ various strategies in an attempt to stop her. These would range from chastising her to cuddling and comforting her. When she was not ritualizing, her parents either would not notice her or would deliberately leave her alone in the hope of not upsetting the temporary cessation of rituals. For example, when leaving for work, Liza would notice that Peta was calm and then would try to sneak out without Peta noticing. Of course, this would increase the likelihood of Peta becoming upset. Thus Peta's anxiety and ritualization was being reinforced by her parents providing her with an increase in attention. Conversely, nonritualizing and engaging in neutral behaviors were ignored by her parents. Thus the family system was adapting to Peta's behavior so that her usual way of communicating her needs in the family was to engage in anxious ritualistic behavior.

Family systems theorists might point to other characteristics of Peta's family that may contribute to the maintenance of the problem. While there are several varieties of theoretical approach that fall under the general banner of family systems theory, the common thread is the idea that the family system can be seen as a functional or homeostatic unit. Disturbance in one family member (the "identified patient") is seen as part of a disturbed family system. At extremes, the identified patient's problems are seen as a symptom that serves to maintain homeostatic balance in an otherwise dysfunctional family. As an example, a child's anxiety may be seen as providing a parent with the feeling that he or she is needed, thereby reducing the likelihood that marital conflict will erupt over a distant and nonintimate marital relationship.

Different schools of thought within psychology and psychiatry emphasize different processes in understanding these disorders. For example, the psychodynamic approach would emphasize factors within Peta's inner world, that is, the conscious and unconscious processes for themes of attachment, intimacy, trust, and need gratification. A biological psychiatrist would also emphasize factors within Peta, but these would be more of a biochemical nature and the resultant treatment would be the use of medication to correct chemical imbalances. Behavioral practitioners would emphasize how the current interpersonal environment has taught and maintains those behaviors in Peta's repertoire. A cognitive therapist would emphasize Peta's cognitive style, her methods for processing information about threat, doubt, and certainty. Family systems theorists would emphasize disturbed processes in the family that may be maintaining the problem.

Although there will be variation in the relative emphasis placed on the family, all of these approaches would agree that the family is one of the most important contexts in which Peta's problems are expressed and maintained. A comprehensive conceptualization and remediation of her problems will need to consider this family context. It is also clear that, in understanding childhood emotional and behavioral disorders, a distinction may need to be made between factors that are associated with the onset of the problem and those involved in the maintenance of the problem.

The rest of this book is dedicated to clarifying the role of the family in disorders such as Peta's. To what extent are the onset and maintenance of childhood behavior disturbances associated with, and explainable in terms of, family functioning? What sort of "tools" can the behavioral sciences use to answer this question, and how much progress has been made in this regard? Is the relationship between Peta's ongoing problems and aspects of the family environment measurable? If so, what sort of assessment strategies can the clinician and scientist use? To what extent do family factors need to be considered in the treatment of childhood behavior problems?

A diversity of theoretical approaches can be readily integrated in the service of answering these questions. These include Patterson's social learning model, Bowlby's attachment theory, Bronfenbenner's ecological model, the internalization models of Vygotsky and others, models of family structure, and contemporary information processing models of Beck, Brewin, and others. All of these theoretical approaches can make unique but complementary contributions to our understanding of how the young child's behavior, emotion, and cognition are both product and architect of the early family system, and how the child internalizes or mentally represents that system into a personal psychology that will determine much of the path in life he or she will take.

DEFINITIONS

The terms *family* and *psychopathology* or *dysfunctional* mean different things to different people. Many authors have struggled with the term *family*, its meaning being highly variable according to the cultural, legal, and contemporary context in which it is used (e.g., see Sussman & Steinmetz, 1987). In this book, a broad definition is used, aiming to include all constellations of people that have one common element: There are one or more adults or adult subsystems that are responsible for one or more children. Thus a *family* is a collection of persons consisting of some mix of generations (parents and children) who, by living arrangements or biological or other ties, form an economic and emotional unit.

The other side of the equation is the emotional and behavioral health of the child or, at the extreme, his or her psychopathology. For the purposes of this book, *dysfunction* will be taken to include behavior, thoughts, and emotions that are distressing to the individual or his or her intimates, prevent the individual from functioning at full potential, and are thought to be caused by some pathological biopsychosocial process.

However, it is impossible to provide one definition of these concepts and achieve the aims of this book. As we will see, the theorizing and research that have been undertaken on families and childhood dysfunction have not been based on a consistent definition of these terms. To be comprehensive, it is necessary to take what is available and employ various definitions as needed. For example, within psychiatry and clinical psychology, it is common for *dysfunction* to be defined in terms of categories of mental illness such as "conduct disorder," "overanxious disorder," "depression," and "autism" (American Psychiatric Association, 1987). These categories of "illness" represent a diagnosis made by a trained clinician. In other research, *dysfunction* is defined and measured according to a child's score on a test reflecting a broad-dimension idea such as "school adjustment" or "internalizing" behavior. In other areas, research is reviewed in which dysfunction in children is defined in terms of the presence of a high rate of one or two troublesome behaviors such as noncompliance with parental and teacher requests or temper tantrums. These various definitions will be adopted as needed. Each has various advantages and disadvantages over the alternatives, and this will be reviewed more thoroughly in Chapter 3.

Finally, an important term in this area is *development*. Dysfunction emerges in children as they develop. Furthermore, the current emphasis on learning in the behavioral sciences assumes that much of this development is due to learning experiences. The recent emergence of the discipline of developmental psychopathology (e.g., Rutter, 1989) has marked one of the most exciting bursts of activity in mental health science. Children change rapidly, and trying to delineate the relationship between "normal" and "abnormal" developmental processes is an extremely challenging task, whether the processes occur within one single child or an entire population of children. Thus the task of assessing the role of the family in the development of dysfunction in children will necessarily entail considering the continuities and discontinuities in behavior, cognition, emotion, and physiology of normal child development as well as the specific variations in these that are associated with the developmental trajectories of common childhood disorders such as conduct problems and anxiety. A general aim of this book then is to introduce the reader to the diverse streams of research and practice that make up this relatively young and exciting science in the hopes of attracting many more creative and humane minds into its service.

In the next chapter, an historical overview of the rise of family models of psychopathology will be presented before a more specific analysis of psychopathology and family processes is considered.

2

THE FAMILY AND PSYCHOPATHOLOGY: AN HISTORICAL OVERVIEW

The idea that children acquire many of their characteristics from learning experiences within the family has truism status in modern thought. So does the idea that problem families produce problem children. The idea that social problems are linked to and thus can be modified by attention to the functioning of families in society goes back at least to the eighteenth century (Thomas & Wilcox, 1987). Given this, it is very surprising to realize that formal theorizing and research into the possible role of the family in the development of mental illness and distress is very recent in the medical and psychological literature. The development of systematic models of family functioning and its influence on children did not really appear until the midpoint of the twentieth century. Still, major textbooks on abnormal psychology devote very little attention to the role of the family in the development of disorder. For example, Rosenhan and Seligman's (1984) classic text only devotes a few pages to the role of the family, specifically focusing on family communication in the etiology of schizophrenia.

In this chapter, a brief history of family models of psychopathology since the early twentieth century is presented. It will emerge that the recent boom in the popularity of many family models and therapies is, in many cases, based on intuitively appealing ideas and assumption, sometimes very sophisticated theory, but often poor quality research; at worst, families—particularly mothers—have been prematurely implicated in the development of the most severe forms of psychopathology. The last few decades have witnessed increasing sophistication in our research strategies, moderation and caution in assigning causal roles to the family, and, consequently, a more sensitive and humane approach to the family in crisis and therapy. We are now at a critical point in the development of family psychology; this chapter has been written in this context.

A number of authors have presented quite detailed histories of the family theory and therapy movement. The current author is indebted to these authors and would refer readers who would like a more comprehensive description to Guerin (1976), Kaslow (1987), and Thomas and Wilcox (1987).

THE EARLY PSYCHODYNAMIC THEORISTS

The contribution of the early twentieth-century psychodynamic theorists to the development of family models is really a negative one in that they created a prevailing paradigm against which the family therapy and social learning movements rebelled. That is, most of the early therapists and theorists who assumed a family approach to their work did so in opposition to the psychodynamic zeitgeist and training they had received. The latter was almost totally focused on the intrapsychic aspects of psychopathology, that is, those that could be localized "within" the psychology of the disturbed person. The principal theoretical constructs emphasized unconscious processes and conflicts that were of biological origin, and thus the prevailing mode of therapy was to consult with the individual sufferer to identify and modify these conflicts. Theorists and practitioners within the emerging areas of marriage counseling, child guidance, family therapy, and behavior therapy shared a common dissatisfaction with the psychodynamic approach in that it provided no conceptual or clinical focus on interactional or interpersonal processes.

THE MARRIAGE AND CHILD
GUIDANCE MOVEMENTS

In the early twentieth century, individual psychoanalytic psychotherapy dominated the landscape of the mental health services, and thus there were no working models for consulting with more than one individual in therapy. The first movement to systematically prescribe dyadic therapy was the marriage guidance movement. Marriage guidance clinics were established in the United States in the 1930s, and the American Association of Marriage Counselors was formed in the 1940s, both emphasizing the assessment and treatment of marital couples as a dyad.

In parallel, these early decades were marked by the development of a number of child guidance clinics and institutes, based on the recognition that childhood behavioral and emotional problems could only be remediated with the support and involvement of the parents. In the early stages of this model, treatment was usually concurrent rather than family based. That is, the parent(s) and the child would be seen concurrently but individually by different clinicians, mostly using psychoanalytic approaches; heavy emphasis was placed on the role of the mother and little effort was expended on systematically involving fathers in helping the child (Kaslow, 1987).

In the 1950s and 1960s, these movements started to merge and an increasing number of therapists experimented with methods of consulting with the family as a whole. Perhaps more important, a number of theorists were viewing social groups, including the family, as systemic or functional units. For example, Parsons (1951) provided an influential text on the analysis of social institutions as "systems" that are both self-regulating and functionally related to their context. The idea of the family as system took hold strongly in the family therapy movement and various therapists argued that mental health problems could only be understood by conducting analysis and therapy at the level of the family system (e.g., Keith & Whitaker, 1982). One of the most influential lines of thought came from theorists and therapists working with schizophrenia.

FAMILY MODELS OF SCHIZOPHRENIA

In the 1950s and 1960s, the dominant interest of family clinicians and theorists was the dynamics of human communication with particular respect to schizophrenia. This is exemplified by the contents of the first edition of the journal *Family Process* (1961), in which the vast majority of articles focused on this disorder and its relationship to interpersonal context. In the United States, Bateson, Jackson, Haley, and Weakland (1956) formulated a "double bind" theory of schizophrenic communication. They hypothesized that schizophrenic behavior was in part a manifestation of family communication that placed the person in a double bind situation. The formal ingredients of such communication are as follows: (a) two or more persons in an intense, codependent relationship, one of whom is the "victim"; (b) a primary negative injunction (e.g., stop acting independently); (c) a secondary injunction that contradicts the first at a more abstract level (e.g., you can't be dependent upon me); (d) a tertiary negative injunction that prohibits the victim from escaping the relationship; (e) the "victim" is unable to comment on the nature of the message being given at a metacommunicative level; (f) finally, the full set of ingredients becomes internalized by the individuals so that they need not all be expressed, and any part of the sequence may be sufficient to precipitate panic or rage. The pattern of conflicting injunctions may even be represented as hallucinatory voices.

In common with most work at the time, the implicated parent was generally the mother. The idea was that the child grows up in a situation where reality is confused, his or her senses cannot be trusted, and there is no escape from the situation.

In Britain in 1964, Laing and Esterson published a descriptive study of the communication styles of seven families with a schizophrenic daughter. They argued that the symptoms of schizophrenia such as thought disorder and sensory confusion, rather than being a set of meaningless symptoms of disturbance, were understandable when one assessed the often bizarre family environments that gave rise to them.

These notions of schizophrenia as a reflection of a disturbed family system rather than a freestanding illness were greeted with scorn from the mainstream psychiatric profession, which was increasingly viewing schizophrenia as a disorder of neurochemical origins (Laing & Esterson, 1974, second edition). Laing and their U.S. colleagues had little to defend themselves with except their own observations: Their studies had not used adequate controls; rarely had quantitative measures been employed; and their samples were not representative. However, these studies were highly influential and the Bateson et al. (1956) paper is frequently cited as a major impetus for the family therapy movement. The influence of these works appears to have had both positive and negative consequences. On the positive side, they were instrumental in forcing a recognition by clinicians and scientists that interpersonal processes, in particular the family, may play a role in the development of psychopathology. On the negative side, these studies were not well designed. They did not employ controls to examine whether families without a schizophrenic member show similar communication patterns; their data were not well quantified; and their samples were not representative. Furthermore, these studies, especially that by Bateson, were part of a tradition within psychiatry that could be seen as blaming mothers for psychological problems in offspring. Bateson was heavily influenced by the Fromm-Reichmann (1948) idea of the schizophrenogenic mother, an idea that can be traced throughout the history of modern psychiatry, that has little empirical support, and that no doubt has caused enormous suffering in the mothers of the mentally ill throughout this century. Despite the revolutionary nature of these ideas, they have done little to promote family-based treatments that have been shown to be effective for schizophrenia.

A related line of research is the work on communication deviance (CD) in families with a schizophrenic member (Singer & Wynne, 1965). This approach hypothesizes that the child becomes disturbed due to internalization of a family communication style that is deficient in the establishment of shared attention and focus of meaning. Generally, this program of research has been more responsive to empirical findings via the use of quantitative analysis of family interaction (Doane, 1985). However, it has not been able to demonstrate that CD is specific to families of schizophrenics compared with families with other forms of psychopathology, and it is not clear whether the communication patterns actually drive the disorder or are themselves a response to the disorder (Doane, 1985).

Research over the last few decades has also identified another characteristic of family environments that is predictive of continuing relapse in people with schizophrenia. Expressed emotion (EE) is generally operationalized as a characteristic of families marked by high levels of criticism directed to the patient by relatives as well as high levels of emotional (over)involvement in the patient's life (Brown, Birley, & Wing, 1972). High EE levels appear to be noxious for the patient in that they predict relapse of positive symptoms and return to hospital (Brown et al., 1972; Vaughn & Leff, 1976). However, EE is not specific to schizophrenia but is a risk factor for ongoing problems in people with a range of disorders, and it appears to develop in response to the disorder rather than as an antecedent (Birchwood & Smith, 1987).

One useful and recent outcome of the EE research has been the parallel development of family intervention programs that appear to lessen the risk of return to florid symptomatology. The conceptual base is the idea that high levels of family intrusion and criticism are noxious for vulnerable people, and that these high levels of criticism reflect two characteristics of families that can be remediated: poor communication skills and lack of knowledge about the illness, which leads the relative to attribute the sufferer's behavior to his or her personality rather than the illness. The latter idea, that the attributions relatives make about the causes and controllability of the patient's behavior may predict outcome for the patient, has recently been discussed (Hooley, 1987) and empirically validated (Brewin, MacCarthy, Duda, & Vaughn, 1991; Harrison, Dadds, Smith, & Baglioni, in press). Treatment programs thus focus on the relatives' knowledge and attributions about the patient's behavior and their ability to communicate effectively with the patient. A growing body of research has demonstrated the efficacy of these programs in improving the outcome of patients with schizophrenia (Falloon et al., 1985).

THE FAMILY AS SYSTEM MOVEMENT

The rise of the family models of schizophrenia led to a huge expansion in the family therapy movement, especially in the United States. In this section, the major schools of thought that share the common view of the family as a system will be introduced and evaluated. Different commentators have identified many different ways of categorizing the different schools of family theory and therapy. These categorizations range in number from Gurman's (1979) three (psychoanalytic, systems, behavioral) to Kaslow's (1987) ten (psychoanalytic, Bowenian, contextual-relational, experiential, problem solving, communicational, structural, strategic-systemic, behavioral, integrative). The aim of this section is not to review all of these schools, as there is considerable overlap and many of them appear to be based on the different personalities and fame of their major proponents rather than any important theoretical or methodological differences. In this section, we will limit the review to psychoanalytic, systems, and structural approaches. The behavioral movement will be discussed separately as it tended to emerge from a different scientific base and has produced far more in terms of empirical exploration and evaluation. In all of the family therapy schools, the common thread is that the family is viewed as system and the family members are viewed as interdependent parts.

The Psychoanalytic Family Movement

One of the earliest pioneers in this approach was Nathan Ackerman, who founded the Family Institute of New York in 1965 but had begun developing his ideas on the importance of the family in psychopathology long before that (see Ackerman, 1938). Practitioners of psychoanalytic family therapy generally approach psychological problems using an integration of psychoanalytic and family systems theory. That is, unconscious factors and one's past history are held to be important, as in traditional psychoanalytic theory. However, these unconscious processes are thought to become manifest in terms of current family processes. Thus the therapist aims to explore each family member's unconscious conflicts at the individual level and in terms of how they are expressed and maintained by current family relationships. For example, in analyzing the marital dyad, the therapist would explore unconscious and conscious reasons for their choice of partners and how this relates to early experiences with parental figures and their current methods for satisfying their emotional and sexual needs.

Techniques that are central to the theory and practice of psychoanalysis are also used in this family approach. For example, *transference* refers to the tendency of patients to transfer their unconscious conflict from their intimates to the therapist during therapy. The therapist will actively encourage this expression of conflicts within the therapist-client relationship so that conflicts can be worked through and resolved in the protected therapeutic environment. In family therapy, the therapist forms a strong relationship with the family on the same premise that the family will thus express deeper conflicts in their relationship with the therapist, thus allowing them to be resolved in that supportive environment.

Gurman (1979) has reviewed a number of the key premises and clinical objectives of psychoanalytic family therapy in terms of mediating goals (e.g., clarification of boundary issues, improvement in open honest expression of feelings, modification of dysfunctional rules, insight into family dynamics, decrease in blaming and coercive interactions) and ultimate goals (e.g., greater trust, closeness, role flexibility, resolution of neurotic conflicts). Readers who would like more detail on the psychoanalytic approach are referred to Gurman (1979) and to Guerin (1976).

Attempts to integrate psychoanalytic theory with family therapies have been very influential and a number of schools of family therapy employ psychoanalytic concepts and terminology (Kaslow, 1987). Some of the major contributions of this approach have been the cross-fertilization of individual and systems approaches, the recognition of the importance of the therapeutic relationship within family therapy, and the recognition that personal history can be important in current family functioning. However, the psychoanalytic approach has had little support empirically. Psychoanalytic concepts are extremely difficult to implement as measurable variables and thus most practitioners have been content to work at the level of theory building and clinical observation. Thus few data are available to support the validity of the psychoanalytic ideas or the effectiveness of their use as a therapeutic tool.

Structural and Systemic Approaches

Structural family therapy was primarily developed by Salvador Minuchin, who trained as a pediatrician in his native country of Argentina but later formalized his structural ideas while working with delinquent children in slum areas of the United States (Minuchin, Montalvo, Guerney, Rosman, & Schumer, 1967). Minuchin and colleagues were interested in the structural characteristics of families that supported delinquency, and later these ideas were applied to families with a member who had eating or other psychological problems (Minuchin & Fishman, 1981).

The major tenet of this school is that behavioral and emotional problems result from structural characteristics of families, and thus changes to an individual's symptoms can be effected by changing the family structures that support these problems. In a broad sense, structure can be thought of as representing the way relationships within the family are organized, especially according to power and family rules. Minuchin sees the family as a rule-governed, hierarchically organized system that comprises a number of important subsystems such as the parental dyad. Individual families develop structures based on implicit rules that regulate individual behavior so as to facilitate daily functioning. These rules vary according to the functional demands placed on the family, but they are seen as maintaining a degree of homeostasis in the system.

Minuchin (1974) contended there are universal and individual rules. Universal rules specify cultural givens such as that parents have more power than children, and that older children should assume more responsibility than younger children. Individual rules develop to regulate the characteristics of specific families, such as "mother handles the financial decisions" or "father does not openly state his wishes, but mother conveys them individually to the children." A combination of universal and individual rules regulate the structure of the family and the behavior of individual members. While these rules maintain the family, flexibility is needed so that the family can adapt to changing circumstances. If a family is unable to employ new patterns, its existence will be challenged when change is forced upon it (e.g., during adolescence, death, relocation).

Family subsystems can be organized along various dimensions such as generation, gender, interests, or functions, and these subsystems, which include the extended family, can overlap, interact, and separate according to the specific demands placed on the family. Thus each family member will belong to several subsystems involving a variety of roles and relationships. Membership in various subsystems and in the family as a whole is regulated by "boundary" rules. Functional families have clear boundaries that allow each individual and subsystem to carry out its roles with a degree of autonomy while maintaining a sense of togetherness with the other members and subsystems (Goldenberg & Goldenberg, 1985; Hayes, 1991). According to structural family therapists, a family becomes dysfunctional when it operates at extremes on a continuum of diffuse and rigid subsystem boundaries. With diffuse boundaries, subsystems are not clearly defined and intrusions from one to another inhibit effective functioning. Families characterized by a lack of role differentiation are called "enmeshed" in this model. Families in which there are rigid boundary rules and thus a lack of open communication are called "disengaged."

The task then of the structural family therapist is to help the family restructure itself to allow for the effective operation of subsystems within the overall structure. For example, Minuchin pointed to the necessity that parents form a subsystem that is hierarchically organized to have executive power over the child subsystems. Structural family models and therapies have become very well known and widely practiced, and a number of the key elements of this approach have been extremely influential. Clearly this model is normative in that it posits how a well-functioning family is structured and, conversely, how dysfunction occurs. Second, this model focuses on the underlying rule structures that lead to daily transactional patterns rather than the transactional patterns themselves. Third, the model takes a homeostatic approach in that it contends that rules are established for the maintenance of the system as a whole. Finally, the model stresses the importance of change. Problems are seen as occurring when the system is challenged by change from within (e.g., a child moves into adolescence and subsequently has demands for autonomy) or from without (e.g., work demands on a parent that change his or her role in the family).

The systemic family therapy model (Haley & Hoffman, 1967; Hoffman, 1981; Selvini-Palazzoli, Boscolo, Cecchin, & Prata, 1978) is similar to the structural approach in that it sees the family as a cybernetic system in which each family member's behavior is interdependent on each other family member, so that a family "whole" exists that is more than the sum of its parts. However, the systemic model rejects the notion of power hierarchies. Rather, each relationship is seen as reflexive and having an equal power of influence in terms of the whole system. The family system, and thus the behavior of individual members, is functionally related in equal proportions to each person in the system, no matter how disengaged they are.

A number of therapy types have evolved within the systemic model and it would be redundant to review them all here. In general, the guiding model is that a family is seen as a whole group and change is aimed at this systemic level by targeting the information in the system for change.

Much of the success of the structural and systemic models comes from the impressive therapeutic style of their major proponents. Demonstrations of Minuchin, Selvini-Palazzoli, Haley, and others working with families have been highly influential due to the active, interventionist role the therapist plays in therapy and the focus on immediate change in the here and now. A number of therapists from other schools have adopted and integrated various structural family therapy techniques into their own models, especially behavior therapies (e.g., Robin & Foster, 1989; Rosenberg, 1978).

This clinical success is, however, contrasted with a lack of empirical validation of key ideas. This is not so much due to failure to find evidence in support of these ideas; rather, good quality research into this area has not been done in sufficient volume to allow any clear conclusions. There is some support for the idea that dysfunctional families are marked by extremes of boundary organization and deviant hierarchical structures in which children exercise more power in the family than parents (Madanes, Duke, & Harbin, 1980). However, as we will see in Chapter 7, this evidence is fairly weak when considered in relation to specific child psychopathology. Furthermore, evidence for the effectiveness of structural and systemic family therapy is generally limited to case descriptions.

Before leaving the history of the family systems movement, a number of the key theoretical points that characterize this movement will be summarized. For readers who wish to obtain a more detailed discussion of the theoretical roots of this movement, the book by Becvar and Becvar (1993) is a comprehensive starting point.

A term that characterizes the theoretical underpinnings of the family systems movement is *cybernetic epistemology*. *Cybernetics* refers to processes of control through feedback. The original Greek *kybernetes* meant a "steersman," and through its Latin evolution it came to mean "governor," a control mechanism or person who keeps a process within certain limits by monitoring and adjusting the behavior of components of the process. For example, most air-conditioning systems have built-in control mechanisms that monitor the temperature and continually adjust the conditioning process to keep the environment within certain specified temperature and humidity ranges. Cybernetics thus incorporates the analysis of information processing, feedback, and control mechanisms in the operation of systems. The earliest writings on cybernetics came from the physical sciences in the early to middle twentieth century (e.g., Wiener, 1948), but these ideas were quickly adopted by the earliest family systems theorists such as Gregory Bateson.

Central ideas within systems theory include recursion or circular causality. Thus the behavior of person A is the logical complement of person

B and vice versa; the stream of behavior is interdependent and reflexive, and is not taken as being caused by any one factor or set of factors in a unidirectional way. Thus, within family systems theory, we replace such linear thinking as "person A is depressed because of ongoing marital problems" with "person A shows depressed behavior in this social situation." Of interest, the family systems theorists often criticize other models of human behavior for not adopting this idea of circular causality. For example, Becvar and Becvar (1993) point to Skinner's behaviorism as an example of linear causal thinking (p. 5). In fact, Skinner and the other behaviorists were explicit that behavior is a constantly evolving stream in which assignment of stimulus and response is arbitrary because causality is circular. Skinner's ideas laid the foundation for a number of family therapies that were firmly based on the idea of interdependence of behavior (e.g., Patterson, 1982).

A second idea central to family systems theory is feedback or self-correction. In this context, the idea of feedback is generally applied at the systems level with reference to the opposed forces of change and stability. That is, the healthy system is able to maintain some stability in the face of change but is also dynamic and evolving despite pressure for sameness. Feedback is the process by which the system maintains itself in a balance of change and stability.

Epistemology refers to the methods by which knowledge is ascertained. In modern empirical science, it is held that knowledge is ascertained through repeated demonstrations of causal relations conducted by "objective" observers. Thus science arrives at truth by having independent observers (scientists, mathematical strategies, measurement devices) replicate dependent relationships between variables. This stands in stark contrast to the phenomenological epistemology adopted by the family systems movement, which assumes that truth is subjective, constructed by individuals and the systems to which they belong. Thus families operate according to their own rules, myths, and logical systems, not any objective reality that can be quantified and objectified.

There are many other concepts and terms that have come to characterize family systems theory, and it would be impossible to cover them all here. Rather, some contemporary issues that face this young approach will be covered. The first concerns the role of family systems theory as a science. The latter half of the twentieth century has witnessed the rise of "scientist practitioner" models of clinical psychology and psychiatry (Hersen & Barlow, 1976). The need for accountability in the face of escalating health care costs has placed enormous pressure on clinicians to evaluate the efficacy of their models of treatments. This is a problem for family systems theory and therapy in that its strength has always been its theoretical richness as opposed to its empirical base. In fact, most family systems theorists reject the modern scientific movement of logical positivism on the grounds that it searches for unidirectional cause, assumes that there can be such a thing as an "objective" observer who is not influenced by the observation system, and assumes an external reality that can be objectively measured. Thus the family systems movement has had little dialogue with the modern empirical sciences of psychology and psychiatry.

The idea that human behavior always occurs in an interdependent system has recently met with criticism from feminists and other commentators on violence and power relationships in society (e.g., Hare-Mustin, 1978). Family system theorists have traditionally seen the behavior of two or more people as mutually caused and interdependent. Sometimes this systemic view speaks of systems in a way that assigns equal power to victims and perpetrators of violence. For example, according to a recent family systems text: "Thus, a sadist requires a masochist, just as a masochist requires a sadist. . . . Similarly, while dominance may look more powerful than submission, one cannot dominate another unless that other agrees to submit" (Becvar & Becvar, 1993, pp. 68-69).

Clearly, sensitivity is needed when applying systems theory to power and violence in interpersonal relationships, otherwise blame can be moved from perpetrators to victims, or at least the system in which they operate. An example of this is the area of systemic models of sexual abuse in families in which fathers have abused daughters. Numerous writers have argued that mothers play a role in maintaining such abusive systems, thereby implicitly removing some of the responsibility from the father perpetrators. The family systems movement has been responsive to the feminist criticisms of its power assumptions and a healthy dialogue has emerged between the two (Becvar & Becvar, 1993).

THE BEHAVIORAL MOVEMENT

The development of behavioral family theory and intervention is closely linked to the history of behavior modification itself. Most commentators recognize two streams in the behavioral family movement: that focused on parent-child relations (e.g., Forehand & Long, 1988; Patterson, 1982; Sanders & Dadds, 1993) and that focused on marital relations (e.g., Jacobsen & Margolin, 1979; Liberman, 1970). Given the focus of this book, the current analysis will be largely restricted to the former area. Traditionally, it has emphasized the importance of social context—that is, parents, teachers, and other significant persons—in the development and treatment of childhood behavior problems (Patterson, 1982; Wahler, 1969).

The application of behavioral theory to the family began as an attempt to apply the laboratory-derived principles of learning of the operant theorists (Skinner, 1953) to children's problems. Early studies were devoted to demonstrating that parents' management practices, in particular the contingencies of reinforcement and punishment, were reliably associated with child problem behavior. For example, Williams (1959) demonstrated that a 21-month-old boy's bedtime tantrum behavior could be eliminated by changing the way parents responded to that behavior. Among other things, these studies clearly demonstrated that such interactions could be measured, and this allowed for the application of experimental designs to the single case (Hersen & Barlow, 1976), which allowed conclusions regarding cause-and-effect relationships between the parent and the child to be made. These early applications of learning theory focused on relatively circumscribed problem behaviors in children. During the 1960s and 1970s, more complex and severe behavioral disturbances began to be investigated; parent training research mushroomed with demonstrations of its efficacy with an increasing range of clinical problems in children. Much of this research supported the basic conclusion that positive changes in specific parent behavior result in a corresponding improvement in the child's behavior and adjustment.

As research and clinical experience with the parent training model increased, and the technology became more widely disseminated, the limitations of a narrowly focused parent training model became apparent. In particular, questions were raised regarding the generalization and maintenance effects of treatment (Forehand & Atkeson, 1977), especially when working with multiproblem families (e.g., Wahler, Leske, & Rogers, 1979), maritally distressed couples (Cole & Morrow, 1981), parents from lower socioeconomic groups (Webster-Stratton, 1985), and depressed parents (Dumas & Wahler, 1983). Thus theorists increasingly stressed the importance of a broader view of the family and the child's social environment in determining behavior (Patterson, 1982), and the use of more ecologically oriented models has been a strong trend within the behavioral family area and psychology in general over the past two decades.

Contemporary family behavior therapists have been highly influenced by Bronfenbrenner's (1977) experimental ecological approach to developmental psychology. He conceived of the ecological environment as a topographically nested arrangement of structures. Each structure has elements that are contained within the next structure. To understand the acquisition and maintenance of problem behaviors within the family from an ecological perspective, research is required at all systems levels (from the individual to the cultural-societal level). A number of authors have applied this ecological model to the behavioral family intervention area (Dadds, 1987; Lutzker, 1984; Wahler & Graves, 1983). An ecobehavioral perspective in the family intervention field fundamentally argues for the importance of considering variables external to the moment-to-moment encounters between parent and child as important determinants of parenting, and hence the child's learning environment. Parental behavior toward children is clearly a function of more than the pattern of antecedent and consequent events children provide contingent upon parental conduct, even though these contingencies are no doubt important. Variables such as a couple's marital interaction, occupational demands and stresses, interactions with relatives and neighbors, psychological state, and the family's financial resources influence, either directly or indirectly, parents' behavior toward their children. For example, a father who works 80 hours a week simply has very little time to devote to child rearing. A mother who experiences frequent criticism from a mother-in-law who looks after a child 3 days a week is exposed to a hostile environment that may be difficult to avoid if alternative care is not readily available.

Wahler has argued that the conceptual basis for understanding family problems needs to be broadened to encompass the wider social context within which the family lives. For example, the research by Wahler and colleagues (e.g., Wahler, 1980) demonstrated that the microprocesses of parent-child interaction were functionally related to more macro variables, such as quality and quantity of social support available to the parent.

Contemporary behavioral approaches to child psychopathology (e.g., Sanders & Dadds, 1993) thus emphasize the integration of micro- and macroprocesses. The former focus heavily on parent-child interactions and the contingencies of reinforcement that occur within them. The latter focus on how these reinforcement patterns are functionally related to the broader family and social characteristics such as marital relations, communication skills, and social support. A main contribution and integrating theme of this approach has been its commitment to empirical evaluation and refinement of its hypotheses and methods.

SUMMARY

The twentieth century has witnessed growth that relates family processes to the development and maintenance of childhood behavioral and emotional problems. The common theme is that the child's behavior is functionally related to the context the family provides for child development. Various schools of thought have focused on the interactional patterns that characterize families, arguing that these patterns carry within them the materials associated with individual disturbance (e.g., double bind communications, reinforcement traps). Other schools have looked at these interactional patterns as a surface manifestation of unresolved intrapersonal conflicts (psychoanalytic) or implicit family rules about structure and subsystem functioning (structural). Clearly, the schools come together on the notion that the individual's behavior is functionally tied to the family context in which it occurs. Causality is seen as circular and complex; to use Gerry Patterson's phrasing, the child is both victim and architect of the family system. This is perhaps one of the most important ideas to come from the social sciences in the twentieth century.

On the negative side, family contexts, and particularly maternal characteristics, have been implicated in the genesis of certain forms of psychopathology, and therapies have been designed based on uncontrolled case studies and theoretical speculation in the absence of empirical support for these ideas. On the more positive side, a rich theoretical heritage has emerged from the application of systems ideas to family functioning. Minuchin's and others' ideas on the structural and systemic characteristics of families are so intuitively appealing as to have been largely accepted with the status of truisms. The application of social learning principles to family processes and problems has led to a clinical science that is firmly rooted in the behavioral sciences, a situation in stark contrast to the vast canyons that typically divide psychological therapies from their corresponding basic science. Methodologically, the behavioral movement stands out as having contributed a rich and diverse set of procedures for measuring family interaction and testing hypotheses using single case and group experimental designs.

In the next two chapters, a more detailed analysis of the current state of knowledge on the role of the family in child psychopathology begins. It will be argued that much progress has occurred in the science of individual characteristics associated with dysfunction and psychopathology. Much of this progress has been ignored by the family therapy movements and thus these movements are in danger of falling behind and becoming outdated.

3

CURRENT ISSUES IN THE PSYCHOPATHOLOGY OF CHILDHOOD

What does it mean to say that a child has an emotional or behavioral disturbance or, at the extreme, that a child has a psychiatric disorder? Recently, attention to the issues of classification of child behavior disturbance has increased dramatically and a number of improvements have occurred. For example, the clarity with which categories are defined is continually being increased such that childhood problems are now classified into five major groups, each with several subcategories, in the *DSM-III-R* (APA, 1987) compared with only adjustment problems and schizophrenia in the first edition of the *DSM.* However, despite these improvements, it is clear that current systems are far from satisfactory (Kazdin, 1988). In this chapter, the current approaches to the taxonomy of child psychopathology will be briefly reviewed followed by a general discussion of their problems and limitations with particular reference to family models of psychopathology.

Categorical systems are based on the long and successful history of medical science in which disease states are classified on the basis of the development of different symptom clusters. Thus diseases can be distinguished and categorized, before an actual cause is known, by careful observation of their clinical manifestation. The two most widely used categorical systems in psychiatry are the *DSM-III-R* classification system (APA, 1987) and the *ICD-9* (WHO, 1992), both of which classify childhood disturbances into symptom clusters that are held to be discrete forms of psychopathology. Roughly, disorders are grouped into developmental disorders, disruptive behavior problems, anxiety disorders, eating disorders, gender problems, tic disorders, toileting problems, and speech problems. One of the main advantages of a categorical system is that it provides a common international language of child psychopathology for researchers and clinicians. However, a taxonomy that assumes discrete types of disorders is fraught with methodological, conceptual, and ethical problems, especially when used at the clinical level, which focuses on individual patterns of psychopathology (Kazdin, 1988). Clinical assessment within the categorical approach is based on the medical tradition of careful examination of the patient by a trained clinician. By interview and observation, the clinician attempts to determine the presence and absence of critical symptoms that are indicative of relevant illness categories. A number of structured interview formats have been developed that correspond to the *DSM-III-R*. These include the Kiddie-SADS (Chambers et al., 1985) for general screening of psychiatric disorder, and a range of structured interviews for specific disorders such as the ADIS for anxiety disorders (Silverman & Nelles, 1988).

The second approach assumes that childhood disturbances, rather than fitting into discrete categories, are best thought of as occurring on a number of nonexclusive dimensions of dysfunction such as aggression, social withdrawal, depression, and anxiety. These dimensions are usually derived from empirical and statistical studies of large populations of children and are found to vary according to the age and sex of the child. This dimensional approach is exemplified by the rating checklists developed by Quay and Peterson (Revised Behavior Problem Checklist; Quay & Peterson, 1983) and Achenbach (Child Behavior Checklist; Achenbach & Edelbrock, 1991). The approach assumes that different disorders vary in the number and intensity of problems children experience. Assessment aims to determine the degree to which a referred child differs from a normative comparison group on constellations of problem dimensions.

The third approach is one that assumes that any attempt to move beyond a detailed description of the actual behaviors a child displays is fraught with methodological and conceptual problems that render it of limited value in treatment planning. Thus the behavioral approach to assessment emphasizes the clear description of the individual case without the inferential process of transforming specific problems to more general diagnostic labels or dimensions of dysfunction (see, for example, Patterson, 1982). All of the above systems have their advantages and disadvantages, in terms of their role both in research and in clinical work with families and children. Each has a useful role to play at the clinical level, and a comprehensive approach should incorporate all three methods at various stages in the assessment and treatment process. This will be emphasized and elaborated upon in the sections describing the assessment of child dysfunction and the discussion of assessment findings with families.

Studies that have examined children in the general population using a categorical approach have found that between 5% and 30% of children meet the criteria for at least one *DSM-III-R* diagnosis (Kashani, Orvaschel, Rosenberg, & Reid, 1989; Rutter et al., 1975). Studies assessing the frequency of psychiatric problems in community samples of 7- to 17-year-olds have found anxiety disorders are the most common diagnosis overall, being slightly more frequent in females but tending to diminish in frequency with age (Garralda & Bailey, 1986; Kashani et al., 1989; Viken, 1985). A number of retrospective studies show that anxious adults report they were anxious children (Dadds, Rapee, & Heard, 1991) and thus it is likely that anxiety problems in childhood are predictive of later problems; however, no prospective longitudinal studies are currently available to confirm these speculations. Anxiety disorders commonly coexist with depression in both adults and children (Brady & Kendall, 1992) and these, together with social withdrawal and psychosomatic complaints, are often referred to as internalizing problems in that the child is seen as acting "in" on him- or herself rather than outward through aggression and impulsivity.

Attention deficit, oppositional, and conduct problems are the next most common overall (Anderson, Williams, McGee, & Silva, 1987; Rutter et al., 1975). These disruptive behavior problems are sometimes called "externalizing" disorders because the child is seen as acting "out" onto the environment in an uncontrolled way. These disorders tend to increase with age from early to middle childhood through adolescence and are the most common referral problems for boys (Kashani et al., 1989; Kazdin, 1987). Furthermore, conduct disorders persist into adulthood for a substantial proportion of children and are predictive of a broader range of adult disorders (Rutter, 1989). The most common complaints with preschool children are disruptive noncompliant behaviors, which are frequent in boys and overall tend to decrease with age until middle childhood. Other common complaints are problems with the child's toileting, eating routines, separation from caregivers, and social withdrawal (Beautrais, Fergusson, & Shannon, 1982; McGuire & Richman, 1986).

Psychopathology and *dysfunction* are changeable and relative terms that not only are difficult to define but are socially "loaded" ideas in that they contain powerful value judgments about the behavior of other people. In particular, the notion of categorical psychopathology is fraught with conceptual, ethical, and methodological difficulties. When we apply the categorical psychopathology approach to children, the picture is even grimmer.

PROBLEMS WITH "PATHOLOGY"

Let us consider the term *psychopathology*. The first set of problems comes from the *pathology* part of the word. Many behaviors that are taken as signs of "pathology" are also present in nonclinical children. For example, lying, stealing, aggression, temper tantrums, and noncompliance are the major behaviors associated with the disruptive behavior problems of conduct disorder and oppositional disorder (APA, 1987). However, these behaviors also occur in most children. Similarly, separation anxiety and fear of new situations and unfamiliar people are common in all children during various phases of their lives; however, these fears also form the basis of two of the most common and debilitating childhood anxiety disorders.

Very often, the difference between a child who has (psycho)pathology and a child who doesn't is based on the frequency, intensity, or developmental age at which the same behaviors are displayed. Separation anxiety and tantrums are common in 2-year-olds but may be a sign of pathology in a 12-year-old. A 4-year-old who throws one or two tantrums per week may be considered normal but a child of similar age who has tantrums every hour may have significant problems. Thus one of the major tasks of the behavioral scientist and clinician is to map the developmental patterns of normal children and how these patterns differ in children who are not functioning well.

Children rarely refer themselves to clinics; parents and teachers are the main referral sources. Thus clinicians are very often dependent upon the observations of these adults when trying to assess and treat a child. This raises the important issues of accuracy of reporting and differences in how different adults perceive and interpret child behavior. This issue is exemplified by a recent study of anxious children. Rapee, Barrett, Dadds, and Evans (in press) examined diagnostic reliability for the *DSM-III-R* categories of overanxious disorder, separation anxiety, avoidant disorder, and simple phobia in a large sample of clinically referred 7- to 14-year-old children. During assessment, one clinician interviewed the parents and another interviewed the child, both using the Anxiety Disorder Interview Schedule for Children (Silverman & Nelles, 1988). As is typical of research in this area, the level of agreement between reports by the parents and reports by the children was very low. Parents were more likely than children to report behaviors consistent with a diagnosis. Furthermore, where children did report problem behaviors, they were more likely to talk about simple phobias (e.g., the dark, animals) rather than behaviors consistent with a more general anxiety diagnosis. Rapee et al. (in press) also asked the clinicians to settle on a "consensus" diagnosis after watching vidcotapes of the separate interviews with the children and the parents. In the majority of cases, the final consensus diagnosis was consistent with the parent's report. Thus relatively little credibility was afforded to the children's reports of their behavior and experiences. An important issue for the categorization of child psychopathology is the source of the information used.

Similarly, a problem associated with defining "pathology" is that definitions of "normal" are highly dependent upon cultural context. The problem of hyperactivity is salient and significant in Western urban children prescribed a daily routine of classrooms and apartments but is largely undefined in many other rural and Third World cultures. Only with longitudinal studies that document the degree to which particular child behaviors such as hyperactivity are predictive of long-term maladjustment will the importance of various child behaviors within their cultural context be discernible.

The categorical approach to psychopathology carries with it the idea that disorders are, to some extent, independent. However, recent research with disturbed children has shown that this is far from the truth. Rather, there is considerable overlap between the disorders as currently defined by the *DSM-III-R*. Anxious children rarely can be diagnosed with one anxiety disorder; the presence of several concurrent anxiety disorders is far more common (Rapee et al., in press). Similarly, the overlaps between anxiety, depression, conduct disorder, oppositional disorder, and attention deficit with hyperactivity are also considerable. The term used to describe this overlap is *comorbidity*; that is, the child has two coexisting morbidities. Of course, there is a problem with circular reasoning in the use of this term. The disorders are defined as categorically distinct. However, when research indicates that it is common for two or more of these disorders to coexist, rather than challenging the notion of the independent category per se, a process of comorbidity is deemed to be operating. That is, the two disorders are still spoken of in a distinct way; the term *comorbidity* assumes a certain covariance between two independent categories.

One viable alternative to this problem of comorbidity is the dimensional approach described above. The dimensional approach assumes that there are a number of empirically verifiable, but overlapping, dimensions of dysfunction such as depression, aggression, anxiety, and impulsivity. A child can score variably on any of these dimensions; there are no assumptions about mutual exclusiveness of behavioral signs and symptoms as there are in the categorical approach. However, this approach has its problems as well. The first is that it does not facilitate communication as well as the categorical approach. Progress is greatly enhanced by a common diagnostic language system for identifying children. It is a lot easier to communicate about a child's diagnosis than about multiple scores on a range of dimensions of dysfunction.

The second problem with the dimensional approach is that its methodology is essentially nomothetic, that is, based on group norms. When assessing a child in this system, the child's scores can only make sense when interpreted against the scores for groups of disturbed and nondisturbed children. Thus, at worst, this system creates a definition of dysfunction based on deviation from the norm rather than on the specific profile of the child's behavior understood within context. No allowance can be made in a pattern of scores for the type and severity of stress that a child has encountered in his or her life, whereas such factors are taken into consideration when making a categorical diagnosis of a child.

PROBLEMS WITH "PSYCHE"

Other conceptual and practical problems come from the *psych* part of *psychopathology,* meaning that the pathology is resident in the "mind" of the child. Even if a broad definition of mind is taken to include behavior, emotion, cognition, and biological processes, there are still problems with assuming the "pathology" exists within the child independent of social context. Theorists in the mid-twentieth century were particularly critical of models of psychopathology that ignored the interpersonal aspects of disorder (see Kaslow, 1987) and, while not without its own methodological and conceptual problems, this interpersonal tradition has led to some productive clinical and theoretical work. A study from the literature on the treatment of childhood pain provides a good example.

Sanders, Rebgetz, et al. (1989, 1990) assessed a behavioral family intervention for children who had recurrent abdominal pain for which a physical cause could not be found. The intervention involved training parents to reinforce the child for pain-free periods, to decrease attention to pain behavior, and to discourage avoidance behavior in the child. The results indicated that the intervention produced significant decreases in the frequency of child pain behaviors, but, more important, the majority of children reported they were no longer experiencing pain after the intervention. Thus the children's pain was highly dependent upon its social context. It could be argued that the pain itself is best conceptualized as an interpersonal rather than an intrapersonal phenomena.

A number of important findings in developmental psychopathology have been made by operationalizing problems in terms of the social context in which they occur and relying heavily on the use of observational assessment to examine them. For example, Patterson's (1982) coercion theory could not have been developed via seeing childhood aggression as residing "within the child." It came from a conceptualization and methodology that saw the conduct problem child's behavior as being firmly seated in an interactional context, that is, within a family system that reciprocates aggression in self-perpetuating, coercive cycles. Support for these ideas was gathered largely through the use of observations of the child interacting with his or her family in natural settings.

A second example comes from the area of depression. For years depression has been "psychologized," that is, seen as residing totally within the psyche or physiology of the depressed person. However, the use of behavioral observations of depressed persons in their natural contexts has indicated that depression is very much context dependent—part of an interactional system, both for adults (Coyne, 1976; Hops et al., 1987) and for children (Cole & Rehm, 1986; Dadds, Sanders, Morrison, & Rebgetz, 1992).

Taking a more interpersonal approach may be especially important in studies of childhood psychopathology for other practical reasons. First, it is possible that children in particular may be limited in their reliability in self-report. In addition, it is not clear that children's language necessarily refers to the same things as adult language. Second, it is likely that contextual factors (especially the family unit) have a far more influential role in the manifestation of childhood disorders than in their adult counterparts. Children have not had as long to internalize their interpretations of the world and their ability to cope, and thus it is likely that they rely far more on significant others for such cues.

SUMMARY

Psychological disturbance and *psychopathology* are problematic terms, especially when used with regard to children. In particular, it is not clear that many forms of behavioral disturbance can be considered pathological or that the disturbance can be considered to reside within the child. Perhaps the best working definition of psychopathology is one that encompasses a broad spectrum of interrelated ideas. When considering whether a child has disturbance worthy of clinical attention, we must consider (a) the frequency, duration, and intensity of behaviors, emotions, thoughts, and physiological processes; (b) the developmental stage of the child who displays these characteristics; (c) the normative developmental patterns of children who are well adjusted; (d) the clustering or covariance of problems that occur; (e) the social context in which they occur, that is, the extent to which the problems are part of an interpersonal system that gives these problems functional value to the child and the system; and (f) the extent to which problems interfere with daily functioning. In what follows, a distinction will not be made between children who have a psychiatric diagnosis and those who have relatively high rates of particular worrisome behaviors such as aggression and fear.

4

MECHANISMS OF THE
DEVELOPMENT OF DYSFUNCTION

The aim of this chapter is to explore the various mechanisms by which psychosocial dysfunction and, at the extreme, psychopathology develop in individuals. The assumption here is that the family, rather than representing some sort of unique mechanism, is a social system in which various mechanisms of influence can operate. Thus it is crucial that researchers and clinicians be knowledgeable of these mechanisms rather than restricting their focus to models of the family per se. A parallel can help to make this point. An environmental scientist contracted to determine the best conditions for the plantation of food crops might compare relative crop growth in various locations to determine the optimum locations. Obviously this would be a very drawn-out and expensive activity; the results would not be forthcoming in the short term and, even if clear differences in location were found, these findings would not be readily generalizable to other locations. There is a far more efficient way of progressing. Suppose the scientist had some idea about what characteristics of soil are important to the crop (e.g., acidity, prevalence of various nutrients). If the scientist had this knowledge of the specific soil and nutrient needs of the crop, he or she could then test the locations for the presence of these factors and the crops could be planted immediately without all the hit-and-miss experimentation.

Similarly, to examine the role of the family in the development of child psychopathology, we need to be very clear about what mechanisms have been identified that are associated with healthy versus unhealthy human development and with increased risk for psychopathology. In this sense, we can relate the presence of these noxious versus protective factors to family functioning as a way of examining the role of families in the development of childhood psychopathology. For example, the social learning models of psychopathology are firmly based on empirically derived models of how organisms learn. Thus the social learning approach to family psychopathology examines the role of general learning mechanisms within the family context.

Many of the family models we reviewed in Chapter 2 have not taken this approach. Rather, they have focused their theories on one or two specific mechanisms, usually derived from clinical observation or theoretical models of how systems work, that are thought to characterize disturbed families and are not generally found in the scientific literature about human learning, development, and psychopathology. For example, the systemic models of family psychopathology talk about mechanisms such as double bind communications that are not found in the general scientific literature on learn ing, human development, and psychopathology. The aim of this chapter is redress this problem with the family literature so as to give it a firmer scientific basis.

There are four sorts of psychosocial models/theories that can be used to shape our thinking about the role of the family. First, there are those that focus on the individual and the vulnerabilities, symptoms, or characteristics that define the dysfunction or psychopathology (subset of general research into the biology and psychology of the individual). In this section, we will consider individual characteristics of both parents and children. Second, there are the theories that describe how people's behavior is functionally interdependent, and thus learning occurs in the context of interpersonal dynamics (subset of general models of social learning theories). Third, there are models of how families in particular are structured and function (subset of general systems theories, group behavior in social psychology). Fourth are the models of how the larger community shapes the previous three (coming from sociology and the relationship of small groups to larger cultural meaning and economic structure). Each has its own contribution to make to the overall picture; all are interdependent, and the family can influence the manifestation of individual dysfunction via any and all of these mechanisms.

CHARACTERISTICS
OF CHILDREN AND PARENTS

Children vary in their vulnerability to behavioral and emotional problems. The review by Rutter et al. (1990) indicated that the evidence of genetic vulnerability differs across different disorders, with autism, major affective disorder, severe delinquency, and multiple tic disorders having a clear genetic component. The evidence with regard to anxiety, oppositional and conduct, substance abuse, and hyperactivity disorders in children, however, is too weak to make any definitive conclusions. Where genetic inheritance predisposes a child to psychological problems, a number of hypotheses regarding the mechanisms of influence exist. Genetic influences may operate through temperamental features, vulnerability to reacting poorly to stress, predisposition for a particular disorder, or through a range of other pathways. Other examples of individual vulnerabilities include behavioral inhibition and anxiety sensitivity, impulsivity, social skills, intelligence, and information processing styles. As was discussed in Chapter 2, a common thread through existing family models and therapies is that causality within systems is circular; that is, the child is both a product and an architect of the family system. Thus it is crucial that family researchers and clinicians be aware of the influence that the child's characteristics can have on the family as well as vice versa.

About 10% of infants have difficult temperaments that make them difficult to rear and place them at risk for later problems (Rutter, 1989). Such infants place extra stress on the family. For example, if an infant cries frequently but cannot be comforted, the parents' attending and comforting behaviors may be extinguished or punished, leading the parent to become less responsive and the child to escalate demanding so as to receive attention (Donovan, Leavitt, & Balling, 1978). The parents may begin to feel very negatively toward the child and themselves; arguments between parents over how best to manage the child may develop and the whole family might start to suffer. A more extreme example can be seen in autism, which is characterized by severe deficits in communication and the presence of bizarre behaviors such as repetitive rocking. Parents of autistic children find that their children do not respond to their attempts to communicate and at intimacy and so the normal parent-child bonds can become severely compromised.

While a difficult temperament places a child at risk for later problems, many children are referred to clinics who may have been "perfect" babies. Furthermore, there is evidence to indicate that a child's temperament is influenced by the family environment during pregnancy and birth. For example, the mother's personal and marital adjustment during pregnancy and her expectations of the child and childbirth experiences all appear to predict the child's later temperament (Scholom, Zucker, & Stollack, 1979; Zeanah, Keener, Stewart, & Anders, 1985). It thus appears that infant temperament and family environment are reciprocally determined from pregnancy onward.

As children enter the school years, a number of other risk factors for psychopathology appear. Learning and language difficulties place the child at risk for behavioral and emotional disturbance (Rutter, 1989). While the mechanisms by which these problems influence the child's adjustment are not fully understood, they clearly compromise the child's development by establishing a pattern of educational, and then occupational, failure and by restricting the social skills and social networks the child can develop (Loeber, 1990; Rutter, 1989). Cognitive factors may also be associated with the development and maintenance of specific disorders. Depressed children show the same negative attributional set about self and others that has repeatedly been observed in depressed adults (Kazdin, 1990). Recent research has also indicated that conduct problem adolescents may be less skilled at interpreting social messages, tending to overdetect, and thus elicit hostility and rejection in other people (Dodge, 1985; Rutter, 1989). Anxious children may be more likely to display behavioral inhibition and social withdrawal (Kagan, Reznick, & Snidman, 1988) and interpret ambiguous situations as threatening (Barrett, Rapee, Dadds, & Ryan, 1993). Many of the above factors may increase the risk for psychopathology by disrupting the developing child's social competence and peer relationships (Parker & Asher, 1987).

The personal adjustment of family members, particularly the parents, has a central impact on the developing child. One of the most widely researched areas of parental adjustment with respect to child psychopathology is maternal depression. Children of depressed mothers have significantly more emotional, somatic, and behavioral problems than children of nondepressed mothers (Billings & Moos, 1983). As with many other stressors, it appears that the effects of maternal depression on the child may be influenced by the marital relationship and the parenting styles and skills of the parents. Thus there exists substantial evidence to indicate that one of the major causes of maternal depression is marital discord (Schaffer, 1985; Waring & Patton, 1984), and Emery, Weintraub, and Neale (1982) found that the effects of a parent's psychopathology on the child were largely ameliorated if the parents had a nondiscordant marriage.

Fathers of severe conduct problem boys show a disproportionately high incidence of antisocial personality disorder, may use severe forms of discipline with their children, and are more likely to be in discordant marriages or to have separated from the family (Lahey et al., 1988). Other factors acting primarily at the level of individual adjustment in families include the presence of a chronically ill or disabled member. Children with these problems, and their siblings, have been shown to be at increased risk for behavioral disturbances (O'Connor & Stachowiak, 1971). Again, there is evidence that the degree of disturbance shown by these children is largely mediated by the quality of the parents' marital relationship and parenting skills (Warren, 1974).

The above are important characteristics that have been shown to be associated with various forms of dysfunction and psychopathology, and family models of psychopathology cannot go on ignoring them. In the past, a number of family therapists and theorists have argued that ideas such as "vulnerability," "depression," "anxiety," and so on are "individualistic" and thus have no place in systemic notions of psychopathology (see Becvar & Becvar, 1993). An approach that emphasizes an integration of individual characteristics and family systems ideas may have the potential, however, to be far more productive than the models that reject individual characteristics. For example, consider the family systems idea of "multifinality," which holds that the same stressor can lead to multiple outcomes, and different stressors can lead to the same outcome (Wilden, 1980). This idea holds that links between family characteristics and child adjustment are nonspecific. It is argued here that, if we incorporate ideas of vulnerability and individual characteristics into family models, it is possible that specific links between family functioning and different types of psychopathology will be uncovered.

INTERPERSONAL DYNAMICS

Many factors affect the child's development but some of the most important processes exist in the interactions of children with their primary caregivers and peers. Even where a child's behavioral adjustment appears to have been adversely affected by an environmental stressor such as a family death or divorce, the stressor affects the child's behavior largely by producing change in the first category, that is, by affecting parent-child relations (Dadds, 1987; Emery, 1982). Major theoretical contributions to understanding parent-child interactions have come from psychoanalytic attachment theory, models of social cognition, and the operant learning paradigm. Each of these approaches offers unique insights into the nature of dyadic relationships, and specifically the role of these in the development of behavioral problems in children.

Bowlby (1973, 1969/1980, 1982), the prominent attachment theorist, integrated the clinical observations of psychoanalysts with an ethological approach usually used by evolutionists and biologists. He drew upon observations of children reared under different degrees of attachment to parental figures such as in orphanages and intact families. He argued that infants are driven to form a small number of stable attachments with other people and that the creation and maintenance of these bonds are necessary for healthy human development. The termination or disruption of these bonds results in displays of ethologically fixed behavior patterns of fear, anger, and despair.

As Brewin (1987) has pointed out, Bowlby's model of how attachment leads to the development of self-esteem is highly consistent with current thinking in experimental cognitive psychology. Bowlby argued that the child appraises new situations and develops behavioral plans guided by mental models of him- or herself and his or her main attachment figures. In healthy human development, these models are gradually integrated into a stable and confident sense of self. Thus Bowlby argued that the disruption of these bonds leads to self-concepts based on anger, fear, and despair, which form the basis of many forms of adult psychopathology.

The idea that loss of attachment bonds is central to the development of psychopathology has met with both theoretical and empirical difficulties (Rutter, 1972). Evidence reviewed in Chapter 6 will show that loss of significant parental figures may pose a general risk for child behavior problems, but it does not appear to be differentially associated with different forms of child psychopathology, and its effect size is generally small compared with other psychosocial factors. However, attachment bonds can vary in many ways other than in the simple loss of them through separation or death of the parent(s). Methods for the assessment of attachment bonds are sufficiently well developed for scientists to examine them under controlled conditions. Ainsworth's (Ainsworth, Blehar, Waters, & Wall, 1978) strange situation test is a method for assessing and categorizing a child's attachment behavior in various challenge situations such as when the parent leaves the child or a stranger approaches the child. While there has been some dispute over the use of these categories of attachment, they appear to be predictive of concurrent and later behavior problems in the child (see Ainsworth, 1989). Recently, measurement of attachment has included self-report forms for use by teenagers and adults to describe current and past relationships. Data resulting from these support Bowlby's predictions that the selection of adult attachments tends to reflect a person's experiences of attachment as a child. Further work is needed to examine the relationships between these bonds, both as they exist in reality and as mental models.

Earlier we discussed how certain cognitive styles appear to characterize various forms of behavioral disturbance. Depressed children tend to anticipate and attend to negative outcomes. Aggressive children may overinterpret hostility in others and thus respond quickly with aggression. Anxious children may overinterpret threat and formulate avoidant plans. Most research has examined these cognitive styles in the individual but increasingly attention is being paid to the interpersonal context of these cognitive styles. That is, researchers are increasingly focusing on how events are interpreted by individuals in relation to their social context. For example, the study by Barrett, Rapee, et al. (1993) showed that anxious children's plans for responding to an ambiguous but potentially threatening social situation are heavily influenced by the way the family discussed the particular problem. In a very creative and well-controlled study, Cole and Rehm (1986) demonstrated that families of depressed children tend to communicate with the depressed children in a way that closely parallels the thinking style of depressed people. That is, the family was particularly attentive to failure and paid little attention to the children's successes.

It is within this context that a reanalysis of Bateson et al.'s (1956) double bind theory of schizophrenia is timely. Recall that these authors specified a form of communication between family members, mostly parents and their psychotic child, that was held to produce anger and panic in the sufferer in the short term, and the extreme confusion and distrust characteristic of psychosis in the longer term. While this theory was revolutionary in the sense that it took mental illness out the individual's psyche and placed it in its interpersonal context, it has not been supported by research into the nature of psychosis. Given the wisdom of hindsight and developments in developmental psychology, it is possible to see that this is probably due to the overspecificity of the theory. That is, it focused too heavily on one type of communication within one relationship context. However, if we think of the double bind hypothesis in a much more general sense, it appears far more powerful and compatible with modern conceptions of child development. That is, children learn to process information about themselves and their environment in the context of their relationship with significant caregivers. The more caregivers model and reinforce confused, contradictory, ambiguous, aggressive, anxious (the list is infinite) interpretations of themselves and the world, the more the child will internalize and use these information processing styles him- or herself. Thus the double bind does not represent some unique communication style that is generative of psychosis but, instead, may represent one of many types of information processing styles that can be transmitted from parents and children and may place a person at risk for emotional and behavioral responses that are maladaptive for the social contexts in which the person has to operate.

The idea that the child internalizes his or her early social context into an emerging cognitive model of reality that is used to interpret and respond to future realities is the hallmark of social developmental theorists such as Vygotsky (1960). Developmentally, the child passes through stages in which behavior is fully dependent on the social context (e.g., child is often lifted up by parents for cuddling and feeding), to an interactional stage in which the child behavior is reciprocal with context (e.g., child can lift arms in anticipation of being lifted up), to a stage when reality is fully internalized into a usable verbal, mental model (e.g., child can abstractly communicate or initiate being picked up by approaching parents with arms raised or using verbal forms).

One of the most productive areas relating the family to child development focuses on the actual moment-to-moment interactions that the family provides as a learning context for children (e.g., Patterson & Reid, 1984). Interactions are conceived of and measured as sequences of discrete but interdependent communicative behaviors. Some very important methodologies and findings have emerged from this approach. For example, observations of families of disruptive and aggressive children in natural environments have shown that members of families that contain aggressive and conduct problem children are more likely to initiate and reciprocate aggressive behaviors than members of families of nonproblem children (Patterson, 1982; Sanders, Dadds, & Bor, 1989). Aggressive behaviors are usually defined to include the use of aversive voice content, tone, and physical aggression. Even during structured home observations by researchers, the occurrence of these conflicts reliably discriminates clinical from nonclinical families (Patterson, 1982). Thus it appears that the families of conduct problem children provide the child with an environment conducive to the learning of a repertoire of aggressive behavior. Similarly, recent research has indicated that parents of depressed children may model depressive behaviors to their children and selectively reinforce cognitions and behaviors associated with depression (Billings & Moos, 1983; Cole & Rehm, 1986).

Studies demonstrating that experimental manipulations of parent behavior result in concomitant changes in aggressive, noncompliant child behaviors have been common in the child behavior therapy literature

(Lochman, 1990). These clinical trials have provided strong evidence of the dependent relationship between oppositional child behavior and inter-actional patterns with parents. Similar evidence exists for recurrent abdominal pain problems (Sanders, Rebgetz, et al., 1989) and some anxiety disorders (Dadds et al., 1991); however, evidence that family changes are reliably associated with improvements in childhood depression has yet to appear.

It appears that disturbed children tend to come from families who engage in relatively high rates of the disturbed behavior themselves in their day-to-day interactions. The aggressive child is regularly exposed to conflicts among family members, is likely to receive high rates of aversive instructions, and many of his or her behaviors will be followed by aversive consequences regardless of their appropriateness. Depressed children are likely to have depressed parents who similarly reinforce the problem in the child. Behavioral conceptualizations of these interactional patterns focus on the functional relationships between individual behaviors. That is, prosocial responses may be punished or ignored while problematic behaviors may be maintained by the consequences they produce.

Patterson (1982) has developed a model for understanding these repetitive family interaction patterns. Reinforcement traps can occur in two ways. First, it is very common to find that parents inadvertently reinforce problematic child behaviors. Consider the following example: Brian, 8 years old, is complaining to his mother that he does not want to do his homework but wants to continue watching TV.

Brian: It's not fair, I hate homework and I want to watch this.

Mother: You know the rule, now get off to your desk (irritated).

Brian: No, it's not fair (starting to cry).

Mother: Come on, I'll help you get started. Get up, please. (Mother starts to pick the child up).

Brian: (Starts to scream and cry) Just let me watch this show, then I promise I'll start then, I promise.

Mother: Alright, just to the end of this show and then you're off to your desk with no fuss. Do you hear me? (yelling).

Brian: Yes, mum.

In this example, Brian's protests are positively reinforced by receiving permission to keep watching and negatively reinforced by the termination of his mother's verbal and physical demands. Simultaneously, the mother is reinforced for giving in by the immediate termination of her son's screaming (negative reinforcement) and the promise of compliance with the new rule about homework (positive reinforcement). Given this inter-action, we would expect the probability that Brian's protests will increase when this scenario next occurs.

There are a number of ways that parents inadvertently reinforce prob-lematic behaviors. Attentional rewards occur when problem child behav-iors produce an increase in parental attention (looking, touching, speak-ing, frowning, smacking, and so on). This is probably the most common and yet inconspicuous reward for problem behavior. Patterson (1982) has clearly demonstrated that child whining and crying results in an immedi-ate increase in parent talking to the child. Material and food rewards are commonly sweets, toys, and other things that parents might give to a child contingent upon certain child behaviors. Activity rewards are when par-ents schedule a pleasant activity as a consequence of problematic child behaviors. Many parents use distraction to a pleasant activity to avoid escalating aggression, demanding, or complaining in their children.

The second way in which a reinforcement trap works is by diminishing the contrast between problematic and desirable child behaviors. The more a child engages in problem behaviors, the less likely the child will be reinforced for positive behaviors. If parents feel they are spending hours engaged in unpleasant interactions with a child (sorting out fights, arguing over chores, having attention demanded), the less likely the parents will notice and attend to positive behaviors by the child. Thus a vicious circle entraps the parent and the child in which the parent has a "break" when-ever the child is not misbehaving, and the child has to escalate problem behaviors to obtain the parent's attention. These examples refer to prob-lem interactions between two persons; however, reinforcement traps can occur in considerably more complex forms. Consider the two following examples from Sanders and Dadds (1993):

> The Davis family are referred because of management problems with their ten year old son who is frequently aggressive, non-compliant, destructive and moody. Assessment reveals that the mother frequently becomes trapped in escalating conflict with son over such issues as chores, homework and choice of friends. The father, however, spends long hours at work and other outside activities and feels that the mother exaggerates the problems with son. On a bad day, the following scenario occurs: During the afternoon, mother and son engage in repeated conflict over chores as they are caught in the reinforce-ment traps described earlier. By the time the father comes home that night, mother is exhausted and feels fed up with son and unsupported by father. She expresses her concerns about the son, but the father is unsympathetic because he feels he should not have to come home to a house full of conflict

and that the mother should be able to manage the problem. However, sometimes the father acquiesces to her wishes and has a long talk with son about his behavior.

All three family members are now caught in a number of reinforcement traps—mother's complaints are aversive to the father and cause him to increase the amount of time he spends away from the family (negative enforcement). The more time the father is away, the more the mother feels unsupported and initiates aversive behavior to son. Thus son is more likely to misbehave with mother, the more likely she is to complain to the father, he withdraws and so on. The son is also intermittently reinforced for misbehavior by receiving a long talk from his otherwise absent father, and by the temporary increase in marital engagement his behavior produces.

Shirley, 32, is a single parent of daughters younger, 5 and older, 11. She has sought help with older who is often angry, sullen and aggressive to her younger sister. Older frequently hits, bites and verbally abuses younger, and often complains that her mother loves her sister more than her. Assessment reveals a common interaction pattern. Usually while Shirley is busy with household chores, a fight will occur between the sisters and escalate quickly to aggression. Mother's enquiries consistently reveal that older has been aggressive and thus the older sister is chastised. The situation repeats itself over the day with the younger sister also increasing her complaints to the mother that she is being picked on, is not loved and so on. Finally, the older sister's aggression becomes intolerable to the mother and the child is sent to bed early. A normal part of Shirley's routine is to read the girls a bedtime story. At first, only younger is read a story but older's crying is more than Shirley can tolerate and she ends the night having a talk with the older sister, reassuring her that she is loved and expressing hope that her behavior will improve.

In this example, both girls are reinforced for fighting because of the attentional rewards it receives from an otherwise occupied mother. Because the older sister is older, bigger and more rapidly provoked into aggression than her sister, she is blamed and punished for the fighting. This is a discriminative stimuli to her signalling that she is unlikely to receive any positive attention from her mother for the next few hours and so the cycle begins again. The younger sister, ostensibly innocent of fighting in the mother's eyes, is reinforced for provoking older to aggression by attentional rewards and increased favoritism she receives from the mother. The mother is reinforced for intervening by the temporary reduction in fighting it produces. Thus the whole pattern escalates through the day until all players are reinforced. Older receives her mother's reassurances of equal love, younger receives her mother's sole attention during the bedtime story, and Shirley has temporarily stopped the conflict and relieved the feelings of guilt that her oldest daughter's complaints evoke in her. (pp. 23-24: Used with permission of the publisher)

STRESSFUL EVENTS

The literature on stress and coping and their relationship to the development of psychopathology is very complex, in part due to inherent ambiguities about the meaning of the terms. It is very difficult to differentiate between stressful events, the stress effects they produce, and the coping strategies that are thought to mediate the relationship between the two. Generally, researchers think about a stressful event as one that produces a stress reaction because the event demands more coping skills than the person has at his or her disposal (Lazarus & Folkman, 1984). Rather than reviewing the large range of possible environmental events that can have adverse effects on children (see Goodyer, 1990), the effects of one common stressor will be used as an example.

The impact of parental divorce and/or separation on the child has been relatively well researched, and marital breakdown affects a substantial proportion of families in most developed countries (Emery, 1982). Children from separated households are at greater risk of developing behavioral and emotional problems than children from intact households (Emery, 1982). Furthermore, recent evidence indicates that reformation of an "intact" family via the remarriage of the sole parent creates even further risk for the behavioral and emotional adjustment of children (Fergusson, Horwood, & Shannon, 1984). There also exists considerable evidence to suggest that a "good" relationship with one of the parents can minimize, but not overcome, the adverse effects of the separation and blending of families on the child.

The effects of divorce on children are largely mediated by the amount and type of conflict between the parents. This is in contrast to psychodynamic explanations of the effects of divorce, which emphasize the direct effects of emotional separation from a parent as the key factor in the impact of divorce on children (Bowlby, 1973). Research emanating from a number of countries and using different methodologies has indicated that it is the discord and not the separation per se that has the most visible effect on the child. Children from broken or intact homes characterized by open marital discord are at greater risk of developing a behavioral disorder than children from broken or intact homes that are relatively nondiscordant. Hetherington, Cox, and Cox (1982) found that the likelihood that the child's behavior would deteriorate following divorce was related to observed changes in the custodial parent's discipline practices. After separation, parents tended to show decreases in their use of limit setting, maturity demands, affection, and clear communication. These were accompanied by increases in disturbed child behavior, which tended to peak approximately 1 year after the event. Furthermore, boys were exposed to more of this inconsistency than were their sisters and were observed to have the most behavioral adjustment problems.

There is also evidence that the effects of severe economic hardship on developing children are mediated by changes in the interactional patterns of parents and their children (Elder, Nguyen, & Caspi, 1985). Furthermore, the established relationship between parental psychopathology and child behavior disorders may also be mediated by the impact of the psychopathology on the marital relationship and related parenting styles (Billings & Moos, 1983; Emery, 1982).

Environmental conditions, in the form of both day-to-day interactions with family members and disruptive events such as divorce, can be important determinants of the development and course of behavior disorders in children. It is clear from the studies cited above that significant amounts of the variance of the effects of disruptive events on children may be accounted for by changes in the interactions the child has with parents concomitant with the event. In the words of Hetherington and Martin (1972):

> The artificiality of separating social learning experiences in the family from extrafamilial social factors, specific traumatic experiences, and hereditary or constitutional factors must be emphasized. Although any one of these factors may initiate a developmental process, unidirectional causality quickly gives way to an interactive process between the child and other family members. (p. 72)

CHARACTERISTICS OF FAMILIES

One of most consistently documented risk factors for pathology, whether physical or psychological, is low socioeconomic status. Poverty is a major health hazard. Its effects do not appear to be related to any specific form of distress; rather, it is a generally noxious factor related to ill health. However, one of the most extensively studied relationships is that of low socioeconomic status (SES) to conduct problems in children. Major steps toward understanding the development of childhood problems, particularly conduct disorders, have recently been made by clarifying the mechanisms by which low SES affects children and families. Social support available to parents may be one important variable mediating the relationship.

Wahler (1980) demonstrated that, in a group of socially isolated mothers with an oppositional child, the number of friendly encounters the parent had with nonfamily members covaried with the occurrence of child behavior problems on a daily basis. Wahler and Afton (1980) showed that the total number of extrafamiliar interactions for mothers was inversely correlated with the total number of parent-child problems, and Wahler, Hughey, and Gordon (1981) found that mothers with low rates of extrafamiliar contact were more likely to engage in longer coercive parent-child interactions than were mothers of oppositional children with higher rates of social contact.

Wahler's conceptualization of these findings draws upon the idea of a perceptual or cognitive bias. As a result of the stress of minimal or aversive social contacts, parents are less able to accurately monitor and label the child's behavior, predisposing them to react aversively to the child in an indiscriminate way. Thus Wahler's research emphasizes an interplay of cognitive, interpersonal, and ecological factors. Others have found support for the existence of a relationship between the adequacy of an individual's support network and ability to deal effectively with personal problems. For example, Lamb and Elster (1985) found that the amount of father engagement with the mother and children was predictive of parental perceptions of social support and of life stressors. Parents who reported inadequate social networks experienced a greater impact of negative life stressors and showed deficits in father-mother and father-child engagement. Webster-Stratton (1985) followed a group of parents for 1 year subsequent to participating in a behavioral treatment program that focused on their children's oppositional behavior. Mothers who maintained a negative perception of the child at follow-up tended to be low SES, single parents who reported high levels of stress during the preceding 12-month period. Comparisons of the components of the low SES status measure revealed, however, that these mothers were no different than the positive-attitude group on measures of income, occupation, and education. The only difference between the groups appeared to be the adequacy of the social support they had during the preceding year.

It appears that factors discussed earlier, such as parent-child interactions, maternal depression, marital discord, and a parent's personal adjustment, may need to be seen in the context of the family's interactions within the system and with the local community. The observation that day-to-day social contacts and subjective evaluations of social support are predictive of a range of parent-parent and parent-child interaction patterns is an excellent example of clinical and research approaches to the analysis of

interacting hierarchical systems (Wahler & Graves, 1983), which emphasize the relationship between "molar" (e.g., SES delinquency) and "molecular" (e.g., parent-child interaction) variables (Patterson & Reid, 1984)

While evidence from controlled studies is generally not available, a
number of other characteristics of family systems are hypothesized to be
important in the development of child psychopathology. One promising
construct is the family systems idea of deviant family hierarchies (Haley,
1976; Minuchin, 1974) in which the parents appear to have less power in
the family than one or more of the children. Using a self-report measure
of family structure—the Family Hierarchy Test (Madanes et al., 1980)—
recent research has shown that families of persons with substance abuse
and conduct problems tend to have more deviant family hierarchies (Green,
Loeber, & Lahey, 1992; Madanes et al., 1980). However, the ability of
this measure of hierarchy to discriminate between other forms of psychopathology is in doubt and the evidence for its reliability and validity is
tenuous (Green et al., 1992).

Importantly, the Green et al. (1992) study found that conduct problems
in a child were predictive of a deviant family hierarchy 1 year later;
however, the reverse was not true. Thus it is likely that family hierarchies
become deviant (i.e., reversed: the child has more power) because of the
child's problems. This is clearly a more simple and appealing explanation
than the reverse logic that a deviant family hierarchy somehow leads to
conduct problems in children. Anyone who has tried either to care for or
to work clinically with the families of teenagers who are on a delinquent
or drug-abusing path will know that their destructive behavior can bring
them enormous interpersonal power, and their parents are often unable to
influence them despite continuous and extreme attempts to do so.

COMMUNITY FACTORS

The twentieth century has witnessed enormous change in the structure
of societies and communities, employment patterns, technology, information transmission, and cultural and religious practices. Many of these changes
may be increasing the stress on children and parents involved in raising
children. In particular, the decline in extended families in most Western
countries may be producing parents who have had few role models for
successful child-rearing techniques and who receive minimal support in
raising children. Single parenting is an increasing social phenomenon, and
90% of single parents are women, who, due to their solo status, may have

relatively low income, support networks, and social status. These conditions may serve to intensify the problems associated with child rearing (Blechman, 1982). Parents in the paid workforce may have less time available to spend with children and may find their parenting at variance with the techniques used by child care personnel. Loss of extended-family supports, worsening of economic conditions, increases in single-parent households, modeling of violence in the media, and the growth of urban overcrowding and isolation may all be contributing to the growing salience of parenting problems.

SUMMARY

Perhaps the earliest identifiable precursor of childhood disorders is the interaction between the temperamental state of the newborn and the psychosocial adjustment of the parents during and after pregnancy. Many childhood problems (oppositional and anxious behavior) grow from the infant's repertoire of distress and nurturance-soliciting signals and, when chronic problems occur, are maintained and shaped within the interactions of the child with his or her caregivers. Social withdrawal and anxious behavior can first be measured as a tendency for infants to become behaviorally inhibited during novel challenge situations and separation from major caregivers, and attachment patterns with parents may be in part responsible for this inhibited style. The establishment of a repertoire of oppositional, depressed, or anxious behaviors may preclude the child from learning more prosocial and problem-solving strategies that protect against psychopathology. Children appear to develop a cognitive style that serves to maintain their problems, and parents may be involved in the development and maintenance of these styles through learning processes. A range of variables are associated with the parents' perceptions of the aversiveness or deviance of their children's behavior and the likelihood that they will engage in conflict with their children. These variables are marital discord, maternal depression, lack of social support, minimal father engagement in family life, and other stressors such as economic disruption, divorce, and the presence of an ill member in the family. The quality of the parental marriage and social support network appears to mediate the effects of stress within and upon the family and child development.

The causes of childhood disorders are best seen as a set of systems, subsystems, and components of systems interacting at the biological, interpersonal, family, and social levels. For family models of child psychopathology and therapy to progress through the next century, they must be seen within and integrated into this general scientific context, just as they implore us to view human behavior within its social context. Family models and therapies will benefit by embracing these rich and diverse scientific disciplines that share an interest in the developmental health of children.

5

MEASUREMENT OF THE CHILD AND FAMILY

One of the main challenges facing a young science is methods for measuring its central concepts. The development of the microscope allowed for enormous progress in the biological sciences as the development of brain scanning apparatuses holds enormous potential for the neurological sciences. By contrast, much of the decline of psychoanalytic thought in the behavioral sciences can be attributed to its central ideas not being amenable to observation and quantification. Similarly, it can be argued that one of the greatest challenges facing the mental health sciences, and family theory and therapy in particular, is the development of measures that will allow scientists to measure family characteristics that are hypothesized to be differentially related to healthy and disturbed human development.

Before a scientist can decide on how to measure family characteristics, he or she must be clear on what it is that should be measured. Why measure this aspect of the family? In the early stages of modern science, a leading British empiricist, Francis Bacon, envisaged vast armies of scientific workers measuring every aspect of nature that could be detected. These data would be scrutinised by scientific overseers charged with discovering the patterns in the data that would reveal the true working of nature. This sort of extreme empiricism is a little naive. Data are of little use unless there is an overriding theoretical structure that provides a context for interpreting them. For example, statistics on the prevalence of childhood depression across different racial and cultural groups may be useful for administrators who are responsible for planning community mental health services. However, these data tell us little about the nature of depression and are thus of little use to the scientist unless they can be interpreted in terms of theoretical models and hypotheses about risk factors for childhood depression.

Clearly, the most important first step in the development of measures is establishing the theoretical basis of our research and clinical questions. The common element of all approaches to the family in psychopathology is the idea that each family member's behavior is interdependent; each member's behavior influences and is, in turn, influenced by other members of the family. Thus the first unit of focus is the dyad. However, all schools of thought recognize that the dyad will be, in turn, influenced by third, fourth, and so on members of the family. Thus it can be argued that the whole is greater than the sum of its parts and thus analysis must also be at the holistic or systemic level. As we move from individual to dyadic to systemic conceptualizations of human behavior, the available measurement technologies become scarcer and less well developed. We will begin by considering the dyad and progress to measuring the family as a unit or system.

DYADIC ASSESSMENT

A number of self-report questionnaires are available that focus on the quality of dyadic relationships. For example, the Spanier Dyadic Adjustment Scale (Spanier, 1976, based on the Locke-Wallace Marital Adjustment Test, 1958) is a self-report measure that measures the quality of marital codependent relationships. A total score on adjustment, and a number of subscale scores, are computed by adding up the items. Some of the items reflect global judgments about the quality of the relationship (e.g., How satisfied are you with your relationship?) and others ask the respondent to rate the presence or absence of specific events (e.g., the number of times you have left your partner).

Similar self-report checklists have been designed for measuring the quality of parent-child relations. For example, the Parental Bonding Inventory (Parker, 1989) was designed for adolescents and adults to retrospectively report on the quality of the parenting they received. The checklist is scored on two dimensions—(a) care and nurturance and (b) overprotectiveness—and research has indicated that the checklist has good psychometric qualities. Similarly, other checklists have been designed for measuring children's perceptions of their parents' marital relationships (Emery & O'Leary, 1982), the amount of social support available from family and friends (Procidano & Heller, 1983), the ability of parents to act as a team in child-rearing duties (Dadds & Powell, 1991), and how family members deal with conflict (Porter & O'Leary, 1980; Straus, 1979). The Parenting Problems Checklist (PPC; Dadds & Powell, 1991) is a 16-item checklist that provides a measure of interparental disagreements over child rearing. The PPC has high internal consistency (alpha = 0.7), and test-retest reliability (0.9), and correlates with both global marital satisfaction and behavioral disturbance in children.

Dyadic relationships can also be assessed via independent observations by third parties. Among the best known of these have been developed by researchers at the Oregon Social Learning Center to measure marital interactions and parent-child interactions. A cornerstone of the behavioral and social interactional approaches to assessment (Patterson & Reid, 1984) is the use of reliable direct observations of the behavior of interest as it occurs in its natural social context. Thus the preference for use of these measures is to conduct observations in the home or community settings in which family problems occur (e.g., Patterson, 1982; Sanders, Dadds, & Bor, 1989).

For example, Patterson (1982) and Sanders, Dadds, and Bor (1989) use a home-based observation in which family members are asked to interact as naturally as possible within the constraints of avoiding visitors, telephone calls, television, and other distractions. A trained observer records the presence or absence of various categories of child and parent behavior and setting events such as location, persons present, and task. Other researchers have chosen more focused settings for observing family interaction. For example, Dadds et al. (1992) conducted observations of family interaction at the evening meal in an attempt to differentiate the types of family interactions associated with depressed, conduct disorder, and nonclinical children.

The degree to which such observations can be successfully used depends upon the observation system employed, the nature of the behaviors of interest and the context within which they occur, and the resources available to the researcher and clinician. As home-based observations are often outside of the resources available to many researchers, a number of strategies have been developed for approximating naturally occurring parent-child interactions in clinic settings. A necessary prerequisite is the availability of one or more rooms equipped with toys suitable for children at various developmental levels, chairs and tables and other props that simulate a family environment, and, preferably, video- or audiotaping equipment or viewing mirrors. Ideally, the clinic setting and the procedure are designed to elicit the problem behaviors and observe the family interaction patterns in which they are embedded (Patterson & Reid, 1984). Furthermore, this needs to be done in a way that best approximates the natural occurrence of these patterns and yet provides sufficient procedural structure to prevent conflict or aggression from escalating to a level that may be unusually distressing for participants.

With young children, a structured parent-child interaction task is particularly useful for sampling a range of parent-child interactions. Where the goal is to sample the immediate antecedents and consequences of child behavior in a short time period, such structure is warranted in that it deliberately directs the parent to interact with the child. Where the clinician is more interested in the natural topography of parent-child interaction, less structure (and more ambiguity) can be useful in providing data on the extent to which the parent structures activities for the child, provides routine, and gives attention.

As children approach middle childhood and adolescence, they become far more conscious of an observer's presence in the home and are less likely to communicate their problems or engage in open conflict with parents and siblings. With older children, it is more important to provide structured guidelines, or select settings, that tend to prompt family interaction. Examples of such settings are family mealtimes and family meetings in which current problems are opened up for general discussion and potential problem solving. Similarly, where problem behaviors are secretive (stealing, truancy, sexual problems) or very low in frequency, direct observation of natural interactions are less likely to provide any useful data, and clinic-based family tasks or sole use of self-report may need to be employed.

A useful procedure that is now commonly used in clinical research on marital distress, parent-adolescent conflict, and family factors in severe psychopathology is the family problem-solving discussion (Miklowitz, Goldstein, Falloon, & Doane, 1984). Such discussions are appropriate for children of approximately 7 to 8 years and older. A number of authors, notably Blechman and McEnroe (1985), emphasize the role of problem-solving competence in protecting a family against conflict and breakdown. The major points for observation are the extent to which family members actively listen to each other's point of view, take time to agree on a problem definition, generate solutions and action strategies, or, conversely, interrupt each other, criticize, talk tangentially, and prevent problem solving through vagueness, concreteness, and expression of hopelessness and despair. The Issues Checklist (Robin, 1981) can be used to generate problems for discussion and is filled out by both parents and child. A recent example of its use was published by Sanders et al. (1992). They compared the discussion in families of depressed, conduct disordered, mixed, and non-clinical children and were able to discriminate between the different families on the basis of the family discussions.

Behaviors vary greatly in their amenability to direct observation. Oppositional behavior in young children, such as crying, noncompliance, and aggression, can be readily observed in the family home or clinic if the setting is selected appropriately. In the home, such behavior tends to escalate at the times when parents attempt to engage young children in routine activities such as bathing, bedtime, getting ready to leave on outings, and mealtimes (Sanders, Dadds, & Bor, 1989). In clinical settings, oppositional behavior will similarly tend to occur when the parent tries to engage the child in structured teaching tasks or when compliance is enforced (e.g., cleaning up toys).

Many problem behaviors, however, cannot be so readily observed. For example, stealing and fire setting tend to be secretive and relatively infrequent behaviors. Similarly, anxious or depressed behaviors may not occur in the presence of the clinician. Furthermore, clinicians are often unable to make home observations due to resource limitations. The use of observational procedures is only limited by the imagination and resources of the clinician or researcher, and the procedures outlined above are just a sample of those commonly used for parent-child problems. Depending on the presenting problem to be assessed, clinic-based analog observations can be used for a diversity of problems. Children with anxiety problems can be assessed in vivo using approach/behavioral avoidance tests (Dadds, Rapee, & Barrett, in press) and a range of analog situations can be structured in the clinic setting to assess social skills problems (Christoff & Myatt, 1987). Recent work in behavioral pediatrics has successfully used observations of clinic-based feeding routines as part of an assessment package for failure to thrive children (Sanders, Patel, Le Gris, & Shepherd, 1990).

Methods for collecting and analyzing data range from qualitative or global ratings made by the clinician to elaborate coding systems that can specify the frequency, intensity, and duration of a set of predefined behaviors. One such method is the Family Observation Schedule (FOS; Sanders, Dadds, & Bor, 1989), one of the many observation systems based on the work of Patterson, Reid, and colleagues (Patterson & Reid, 1984). The frequencies of these behaviors, in particular the aversive categories of parent and child behavior, have been shown to discriminate between distressed and nondistressed families (Sanders, Dadds, & Bor, 1989).

It should be noted that the methods discussed above typically are used to observe the occurrence of behaviors in each *individual* within the family context. The dyadic aspects of the interaction are included within the behavioral definitions themselves. For example, most observation systems for young children use a category of child noncompliance, which is scored when the child does not comply with an adult directive within a certain time period. Thus, while the actual behavior is scored against the child, the definition is clearly inclusive of the antecedent parent behavior. The parent's frequency of different types of instruction will also be scored (e.g., Forehand & Long, 1988) and thus analysis of the data can include, for example, associations between parent instructions and child compliance.

However, this sort of analysis does not allow researchers to describe the specific sequences and interdependencies of behavior that occur on a moment-to-moment basis within families. When quantitative methods are used, the main problem to overcome is how to represent complex and often fast moving sequences of behavior as useful, meaningful data. A recent innovation in behavioral assessment has been the development of computerized observation and analysis systems that allow the clinician to test hypotheses about conditional probabilities of interrelated sequences of family behavior (e.g., Dumas, 1989). In this type of analysis, the ongoing interactional sequence is divided into behavioral units; for example, each utterance might be regarded as a behavioral unit. Each unit is then classified according to a categorization system that reflects the researcher's research questions and hypotheses.

The researcher can then analyze an interactional sequence by frequency counts or conditional probabilities. Frequency counts are simply tallies of how often each person engages in a particular behavioral unit or category, usually expressed as a percentage of the total number of units observed. Conditional probability analyses go a step further by attempting to describe interdependencies between different persons' behaviors. First, the base rate of a particular behavior of interest is calculated and expressed as a probability. This probability is then compared against the probability of the same behavior given that it was preceded by another behavior of interest. A z statistic is used to test whether the two probabilities are reliably different than each other.

Consider the following example. A family therapist is interested in examining the relationship between marital communication and child oppositional behavior. Hypothesizing that a child's oppositional behavior functions in part to terminate marital conflict, families are videotaped while interacting. Instances of marital conflict are coded, as are instances of oppositional behavior, and then base rate probabilities are calculated for each. If the probability of the child engaging in oppositional behavior following instances of marital conflict is significantly greater than the probability of the child being oppositional in general, then the researcher has demonstrated that child oppositional behavior is functionally dependent on marital conflict. If the probability of marital conflict diminishes given that the child has just engaged in oppositional behavior, it appears that the hypothesis has been supported. That is, the child's oppositional behavior serves to terminate marital problems.

This system of observation and probability analysis is in its infancy but holds enormous potential for the description of complex interactional systems. Many of the hypotheses emanating from the family systems and behavioral models could be explored and tested using this methodology; however, few researchers have taken up this challenge. It is hoped that the next few decades will witness increasing use of these sequential models. Interested readers can find more detail in Dumas (1989).

ASSESSING CHARACTERISTICS OF SYSTEMS

Assessing the characteristics of a system such as a family involves obtaining measures on the structure and process of the system over and above its individual members or dyadic relationships. This can be done by self-report or observational measures. Most of the attempts to assess family systems have used classification systems in which the goal of assessment is to identify families with reference to fixed typologies. For example, Kantor and Lehr (1975) developed a system in which families were classified as "open," "closed," or "random." As with all typologies, however, Kantor and Lehr acknowledged that no family could be a pure type and that considerable overlap occurs.

In parallel to the *DSM-III* approach of the American Psychiatric Association, Tseng and McDermott (1979) developed a multiaxial approach to family assessment in which family is assessed on three interdependent dimensions. Axis 1: Family developmental dysfunction includes problems that the family has had negotiating common developmental milestones such as the birth of a child and adolescent autonomy. Axis 2: Family subsystem dysfunction includes dysfunction in parent-parent and parent-child subsystems; and Axis 3 includes problems at the broader family systems level (e.g., rigidity, reversed hierarchies) and social interaction level (e.g., social isolation, cultural problems). Tseng and McDermott's (1979) model is based on the skill of the clinician in using the system, as it provides no objective guidelines. As such, it is a framework for structuring an assessment rather than a set of criteria or strategies for describing families. It is important though in its attempt to incorporate multiple levels of family functioning in a single comprehensive assessment strategy.

Two of the best known self-report measures of family functioning are the Family Adaptability and Cohesion Scale (FACES; Olson, Portner, & Bell, 1982) and the Family Environment Scale (FES; Moos, 1974). Both of these scales involve family members making ratings about the way the family interacts and communicates, and can be completed by parents as well as children and adolescents. The FACES assessment is based on the structural theories of Minuchin and the circumplex model of Olson, Russell, and Sprenkle (1983) in which families are classified on two orthogonal dimensions: cohesion and adaptability. Families can be classified in four categories on each dimension, namely, cohesion (disengaged, separated, connected, enmeshed) and adaptability (rigid, structured, flexible, chaotic), giving up to 16 categories. According to this model, healthy family functioning relates to balance on these major dimensions. That is, the family can move in a balanced way between disengagement and enmeshment, and stability and change.

The Family Hierarchy Test (Madanes et al., 1980; Madden & Harbin, 1983) is a self-report measure designed to assess the presence or absence of deviant family hierarchies. Based on the hypotheses of structural family therapy (Haley, 1976; Minuchin, 1974) that child psychopathology is associated with family structures in which children exercise more power in families than do parents, the test obtains family representations from individual family members about their hierarchical organization, in particular the presence of child domination.

Research has indicated that reversed hierarchies are reliably associated with substance abuse in offspring (Green, 1992; Madanes et al., 1980). However, the evidence for the temporal stability of the measure is tenuous, little agreement is found with parental and child reports of family structure, and its ability to discriminate between various forms of child psychopathology appears limited (Green et al., 1992). An additional important finding of the Green et al. (1992) study was that conduct problems in the child predicted a deviant family hierarchy 1 year later, but the reverse was not true. Thus these data point to the powerful effects of the child's problems on the family in contrast to the usual focus on the child's problems as a result of family problems.

Another recent example is the Family Systems Test (Gehring & Marti, 1993). There are many assessment strategies for families and only the most widely used and known have been covered here. Readers interested in more comprehensive accounts are referred to Touliatos, Perlmutter, and Strauss (1990).

Unfortunately, observational methods for assessing characteristics of systems are still in their infancy. Rating scales have been developed on which an independent observer makes global judgments about various aspects of the family. For example, the FACES scale can be used by a clinician to make ratings of a family (Olson et al., 1982); however, at this time, few data are available to support the reliability and validity of this measure.

Similarly, a number of research projects have asked independent raters to make global judgments about various aspects of families. For example, Julien, Markman, and Lindahl (1989) found that global ratings of marital interactions were able to discriminate between distressed and nondistressed couples. Robin and Canter (1984) found that global ratings of family interaction were significantly correlated with parallel measures derived from microcoding systems.

Observational systems in which independent observers record the specific instances of family transactions, over and above the behavior of individual members, are rare. Some notable examples include the research by Singer, Wing, and colleagues, who developed systems for observing communication styles in families with a member with psychosis (see the review by Doane, 1985). In a study of the relationship between marital interactions and child oppositional behavior, Dadds, Sanders, Behrens, and James (1987) observed four families who had marital problems and a child with oppositional disorder in the home setting throughout their participation in a family therapy program. Observations were coded at the dyadic level, that is, parent-child and parent-parent interactions. However, by analyzing the concurrent variations in the parent-child and parent-parent interactions, these authors were able to identify several functional relationships between the marital dyad and the parent-child dyads.

Clearly, one of the most important areas of progress needed is the development of new and reliable methods for observing family interactions in ways that allow analysis of triadic and systemic constructs.

SOME ISSUES IN ASSESSMENT

Most of the earliest psychological assessment strategies for use with individuals and families arose within the psychoanalytic movement as a way of accessing a person's unconscious conflicts. Examples are the

Rorschach inkblot test in which the respondent is asked to say what he or she sees in a vague inkblot shape or the Thematic Apperception Test in which the respondent is asked to interpret a series of ambiguous pictures of people in various situations. There have been concerted efforts to standardize the scoring and interpretation of these tests (e.g., Holtzman, 1976); however, they largely remain open to the interpretation of the individual using them and thus have had little use in research and clinical work that seeks to be replicable.

Despite this significant limitation, there are some ideas associated with these interpretative tests that may still have potential for the child and family area. First, it is sometimes very difficult to obtain information about the thoughts and feelings of young children or children who cannot or will not express themselves directly to clinicians. Asking the child to respond to ambiguous stimuli such as are found in these tests may be a nonthreatening way of encouraging a child to express him- or herself. Additional work should be done to refine the reliability and validity of such methods. Second, the provision of ambiguous stimuli has been successfully used as a way of focusing a family's attention and assessing the ways in which they communicate, problem solve, and influence each other's way of thinking. For example, Singer, Wing, and colleagues used this method in their analyses of family interaction and schizophrenia, and this tradition has been successfully generalized into the communication deviance and expressed emotion areas (see Doane, 1985).

Third, the provision of an ambiguous stimulus can elicit cognitive processing styles that may be characteristic of particular forms of distress such as anxiety and depression. For example, a number of researchers have recently proposed the hypothesis that the maintenance of anxiety disorders may in part be explained by a cognitive bias toward perceiving threat in the environment (Brewin, 1987). The most common way of assessing this is to present the subject with a series of ambiguous situations that could be perceived as containing a threatening situation and to ask for an interpretation. The dependent variable is the percentage of threat interpretations made by the subject. Recent applications of this research paradigm to the anxiety disorders (Barrett, Rapee, et al., 1993) indicate it may have great potential for elucidating information processing styles in children and families.

Since the middle of the twentieth century, many assessment strategies have been "behavioral" in that they ask respondents simply to rate characteristics of observable behavior, thoughts, and feelings, usually in the form of checklists and behavioral rating forms. For example, the Beck

Depression Inventory (Beck et al., 1961) asks respondents to check off the presence of a number of behaviors, thoughts, feelings, and bodily changes associated with depression (e.g., low mood, suicidal thoughts, weight loss). In the child area, the CBC (Achenbach & Edelbrock, 1991) asks parents to check off the presence or absence of a number of child behaviors held to be indicative of dysfunction. Both of these checklists can be scored and compared with scores found in a range of clinical and normative samples. However, individual items can also be interpreted as there is no inferential leap to be made by the clinician; the item simply provides a report about the presence of a behavior. These checklist-type measures are now the status quo in assessment of distress and disturbance and have contributed much toward the refinement of measurement technology. However, in the child and family area, the thorny issue of whose reports should be considered valid is particularly salient in the use of these report forms. Can family members accurately report on subtle characteristics of the family? Typically, children below about 7 years of age are not able to make reliable reports of their behavior and experiences, and there are very few checklists for use with children below this age.

Observing the child and family in the home or the community has the potential to produce the most ecologically valid data. That is, we would expect that observations in these settings would give us the most accurate sample of the child's and family's daily behavior. Furthermore, these observations allow the observer to sample aspects of the setting, such as space, routines, crowding, noise level, and safety, that may be functionally related to the child's problems (e.g., Lutzker, 1984; Sanders, Dadds, et al., 1989). However, observations in natural settings are often expensive and, of course, not conducive to the collection of highly reliable data unless considerable skill is applied to the design of the observational system and the training of observers. It has long been a part of the research folklore with children and families that clinic-based assessments are not as valid as home settings, the latter being regarded as "naturalistic." This may well be an exaggeration of the differences, however. Taking children into a community setting such as a health clinic is a regular occurrence for families and often one that is associated with major child management difficulties (Sanders, Dadds, et al., 1989). Children are often very difficult to manage in these environments and thus the clinic setting can elicit good examples of family interaction problems. Even when certain family members refuse to attend a clinic, this is no doubt indicative of the way a family structures the responsibilities of individual members.

The nature of the setting in which families are observed and the tasks they are given to facilitate interaction are important variables that will influence the family style. A study by Terkelson (1983) showed that exposing a family to a therapist who had a family systems outlook tended to produce deviant family interaction patterns, probably because the family could sense that their family style was under scrutiny as a causal factor in the child's problems. Research is needed to delineate critical setting and task factors associated with the escalation and diminution of important family processes such as problem solving, anxiety, and aggression.

One of the major tools of scientific progress is objective measurement; however, people are not generally reliable witnesses. In the family area, many models are based on concepts that may be difficult to measure reliably across different subjects, observers, and research clinics. Reliability of our measures is thus a critical issue and, given that observation of behavior involves subjective decisions, it is important to have two (or more) observers so as to randomize the error associated with any measurement or so that interrater reliability can be assessed. Sources of error coming from observers are well documented and include the following: (a) *Observer expectancy and bias:* Observers will tend to produce data that are consistent with their expectations of what they "should" see. Thus it is important that observers remain unaware of experimental hypotheses, are not given feedback about the content of their data, and are not put under any pressure, however subtle, to observe what experimenters want them to see. (b) *Observer drift:* Observers tend to alter the way they observe behavior over time. Thus all observation systems that extend in time should build in observer retraining sessions in which the observers are intermittently "recalibrated" to the observation system.

Interrater reliability data are collected by having two or more observers conduct parallel observations of the same situation, usually on at least 20% or more of all observations conducted. Summary statistics on interobserver reliability are then calculated for each behavior category under each experimental condition. For discrete behaviors and interval time sampling, this should be done using percentage agreement for both occurrences and nonoccurrences of the behavior adjusted for chance with an appropriate statistic such as Cohen's kappa. For global ratings, interobserver agreement is usually presented in terms of simple correlations between the two observers' ratings. Additional information on the theory and practice of interobserver agreement can be found in Ollendick and Hersen (1984).

Psychological and behavioral phenomena are very difficult to measure and each system of measurement has inherent source errors that are unique to that system and also shared with all other measurement systems. To reduce error that is unique to any one system, multiple measurement systems can be employed. As we have seen, little evidence is available to support the external validity of current systems for observing anxiety in children. That is, we are not exactly sure what they are measuring. Thus it is wise to always include multiple forms of measurement, examine the degree of convergence between measures, and draw conclusions that are not limited to one method of assessment.

SUMMARY

Accurate measurement is a critical factor in the development of all sciences. The absence of good measures is a critical factor limiting progress in the child and family area. As we move from measures of individual to dyadic to triadic and systemic processes, the quality of the available measures rapidly diminishes. However, some creative opportunities exist for development. In particular, more reliable self-report measures of characteristics of family systems are needed. Second, the use of global or subjective ratings of family processes by independent observers appears to yield reliable, valid, and inexpensive data that can capture highly subtle aspects of family systems. Third, direct observation strategies with families are increasingly able to capture the complexity and subtlety of family processes due to developments in task and setting selection, direct observation and coding procedures, and the use of sequential and conditional probability analyses.

6

RESEARCH DESIGNS
WITH FAMILIES AND CHILDREN

So far we have covered the history of family therapy and the current status of our knowledge of child psychopathology. In the last chapter, methods for measuring characteristics of children and families were discussed. Thus the next general aim is to explore the scientific substance of this area, that is, to review findings about the role of families in the development of the major childhood behavioral and emotional problems. To do this in a critical and scholarly way, we must understand that research findings vary considerably in quality. To truly appreciate the worth of scientific findings, one must understand the methodologies that have produced them. Thus the aim of this chapter is to review the common methods for establishing reliable associations between family variables and child psychopathology. In the next chapter, substantive evidence about the relationship of family variables to common childhood problems, specifically depression, conduct disorder, anxiety, and somatic complaints, will be reviewed using a framework based on these different research methodologies.

The reason for conducting an analysis of research design logic is that this issue is timely and critical. In Chapter 3, it was argued that the mental health sciences have a mixed record when it comes to family-based models of mental illness. Within the latter half of the twentieth century, we have embraced theories and therapies that, either explicitly or implicitly, have ascribed blame to families for many different forms of psychopathology. These models have generally been based on very basic scientific mistakes, the most common being not using appropriate controls. Characteristics that appeared specific to families of persons with mental illness were later found to be common to other illnesses and even families with no illness. Other lines of research and reasoning have led to productive methodologies, findings, and treatments. As the close of this century draws near, it is imperative that we make substantive improvements in our methodologies or risk carrying a partial legacy of speculation into the next.

METHODS FOR STUDYING FAMILIES AND CHILD PSYCHOPATHOLOGY

The Case Study

The case study is perhaps the oldest and most common methodology that has shaped current thinking about the role of the family in child psychopathology. Based on the tradition of the physician making careful observations of the patient and his or her illness, the case study is dependent upon the observational skills of the clinician. The validity and reliability of these observations are established by replication across multiple clinicians and patients with the same disorder.

Within the area of the family and child psychopathology, some of the most influential ideas of this century have come from this observational method. Freud's description of little Hans provided one of the first models of anxiety in children. Hans had an extreme fear of leaving the safety of his home and parents' company. The fear began after Hans witnessed a violent scene on the street in which a horse fell and was violently punished by its owner. Freud interpreted Hans's fear in terms of Oedipal dynamics in which Hans was frightened to return to the street because the violent scene he had witnessed provoked his own unconscious feelings of competitiveness and violence toward his father. The early American behaviorists Watson and Raynor (1924) described work with another child, little Albert, who learned to fear a rabbit after repeated pairings of the rabbit and a loud noise in Watson's laboratory. Thus the behaviorists countered Freud's explanation of the development of fear with their own demonstration of a classical conditioning explanation of fear.

Of interest, subsequent research has provided little support for either explanation. That is, there are few data and, in fact, few methodologies that can support the Oedipal model of anxiety, and attempts to replicate Watson and Raynor's demonstration of phobias learned in a laboratory have largely been unsuccessful. Despite these failures, these two clinical descriptions, essentially case studies, continue to be highly influential as landmark developments in clinical psychology and psychiatry.

In the middle of the twentieth century, a plethora of case studies were published that aimed to develop and provide support for a family-based model of schizophrenia. Laing and Esterson (1964/1974), for example, based a psychosocial model of schizophrenia on observations of the communication patterns of several schizophrenic patients and their parents. These and other highly influential models of schizophrenia and the family (e.g., Bateson et al., 1956) were largely based on uncontrolled clinical case observations, although exceptions that used more sophisticated methodologies did exist (e.g., Singer & Wynne, 1965).

Through the latter half of this century, the case description has continued as a common form of presenting ideas about the nature and treatment of psychopathology. Because of the increasing interest in the social, especially familial, context of psychopathology, case studies have increasingly included descriptions of the family as well as the identified patient. For example, Atoynatan (1986) presented an overview of elective mutism in children, which, based on case observation and psychodynamic theory, places heavy emphasis on the role of the family, especially the mother, in perpetuating this problem in the child.

Due to the influential nature of case studies, clinical folklore develops about particular disorders and the best ways to manage them. For example, the families of anorexics have a certain image in the psychotherapeutic world, usually of a rigid and domineering father, an unassertive mother, and a sensitive but rebellious child in a rigid, enmeshed family system. Families of conduct problem boys are widely thought of as chaotic, disengaged, of low socioeconomic status, and aggressive. Most of this folklore comes from case studies. Despite the highly influential nature of this method, its value as a scientific tool is limited. The main advantage is that the case study is probably one of the most creative sources of new ideas about families and psychopathology. At worst, it is an uncontrolled method that reflects the biases of the clinician observer rather than any truth about the phenomena it seeks to illuminate.

Case studies provide a wealth of interesting material and can generate new ideas and hypotheses that can then be tested by more rigorous experimental designs. The majority of case studies are uncontrolled, and thus the main limitation of this approach is that the worth of the study is largely dependent on the skills and credibility of the author-clinician. However, there exists a well-developed methodology that can be applied to single cases that allows the scientist-clinician to assess relationships between independent and dependent variables using traditional experimental manipulations. Referred to as "single case experimental designs" (Hersen & Barlow, 1976), these designs largely have been employed only by behaviorally oriented clinicians. This is to be regretted as these designs have the potential to be used to evaluate a range of interventions, including medical, dietary, psychodynamic, and family systems, for the single case or family.

Correlational Designs

Correlational studies examine the extent to which two or more variables are related to each other. Cigarette smoking and heart disease are positively correlated, age of children and frequency of toileting problems are negatively correlated, and rainfall in the United States and length of men's hair in Europe are (probably) uncorrelated variables. Thus a correlation tells us the extent to which two or more variables are associated or tend to change together. This is a very useful technique, as will be discussed. However, it has two very important limitations.

First, a correlation is a descriptive index of how two variables are related based on multiple observations. For example, to calculate the correlation between height and weight, we would need to take measures of these variables in a large sample of persons. The correlation will tell us the strength of the association, and the more people we assess, the more accurate our correlation will be. However, the correlation tells us little about the relationship between height and weight in any individual. Knowing that someone is short will lead us to guess that his weight is relatively low, but, based on a group correlation, there is no way that we can be sure of this for any particular individual.

Second, correlations do not imply causality. The frequency of thunder and lightning across a given time period would be highly correlated variables. However, this does not mean that thunder causes lightning or vice versa. Both thunder and lightning are caused by other variables: the collision of two atmospheric masses, different electrical charges, and so on. Third, there is the problem of method variance in which variables can be found to correlate simply because they have been measured using the same method. For example, collecting self-report measures exclusively from parents will inflate correlations simply because the same person is following the same procedure across measures. Researchers need to use multiple informants and different procedures (self-report, direct observation, multiple raters) to overcome this problem.

These limitations of correlational designs are very important for the area of child and family mental health because more rigorous experimental designs are not often ethically or practically possible. For example, it has been repeatedly shown that marital problems of parents correlate with behavioral problems in offspring (Emery, 1982). However, this does not imply that the former causes the latter or vice versa. Furthermore, it does not imply that, for any one particular family, a discordant marriage will have an adverse effect on the children. More sophisticated designs are needed to clarify these issues. Where a correlation between two variables is established, it is impossible to know whether their relationship is in fact a product of a third variable. Thus the presentation of simple correlations can lead to very oversimplistic and erroneous conclusions unless suitable controls are exercised. Two of the most important contextual controls on the interpretation of correlations are a precise theoretical formulation and the simultaneous consideration of possible confounding variables. That is, a correlation is useful only to the extent that it relates to theory. Theories specify the interrelationships of multiple variables and thus any variables that might mediate or confound the relationship of interest need to be considered and controlled.

An example comes from Lahey et al. (1988). Many researchers had shown that marital problems were correlated with conduct problems in children. Lahey et al. (1988) showed that both conduct problems in children and marital problems in parents were correlated with antisocialness problems in fathers. When the level of antisocial behavior in fathers was controlled, the correlation between marital problems in parents and conduct problems in children greatly diminished. Notwithstanding, when used appropriately, this design has made and will continue to make an important contribution to the area of child psychology and the family. Considerable progress will be made by improving our use of correlational designs to overcome method variance and to control for confounds in the context of multivariate models of child behavior and family relations.

Group Comparison Designs

Typical group comparison designs seek to compare the families of children with behavioral and emotional problems with families of children with no problems or with different problems. Because the independent variable (diagnostic status) is produced by selection rather than manipulation, these are correlational rather than experimental designs and the researcher cannot be sure that the differences are due to the independent variable rather than some other confounding variable.

An example is the recent study by Gehring and Marti (1993) in which a heterogeneous group of clinically referred children were compared with a nonclinical sample on their responses to the Family Systems Test. Differences between the clinical and nonclinical children were found and the authors thus concluded that the test is sensitive to characteristics of family systems of disturbed children that differentiate them from nondisturbed children. However, closer inspection of their paper reveals that these conclusions are not allowable in terms of the methodology used. No data are presented on the equivalence of the clinical and nonclinical groups on possible confounding variables. Socioeconomic status, education level, frequencies of single-parent families and stepfamilies, and age and sex of the child are examples of important variables that are predictive of family relations but are not considered in this paper. Thus it is impossible to discern if the results are due to other factors that differentiate the groups.

Sampling problems are also affected by inclusion and exclusion criteria. In the Gehring and Marti study, children with family members who showed chronic medical problems, mental disorders, deviance, or disability were excluded from the study. It appears that this exclusion criterion was applied to the nonclinical group only and thus any conclusions about differences between families in the two groups may be erroneous. Furthermore, nonclinical or control samples are often volunteers who are recruited from a community setting. Thus they do not represent an ideal control in that differences between the groups could be due to factors associated with the self-selection process that occurs when sampling is based on volunteering (see Badia, Huber, & Runyon, 1970).

Perhaps more important is the issue of what group comparison studies mean even when differences between the groups are found. What does it mean to show that families of children in clinics are different than families of children not in clinics? Very little, unless the selection of control groups is done very carefully. The effects could be due to the stress of clinic presentation itself. Previous research has pointed to possible adverse effects of family assessment and treatment on family process (e.g., Terkelson, 1983). The only way to overcome this problem is to employ more appropriate control groups, that is, children and families who are presenting clinically about a problem that is not substantially related to family relations, such as families with acute medical conditions.

Group comparison designs are common and economical but vary highly in quality according to the specifics of group formation. In particular, attention needs to be paid to the choice of appropriate control groups, the delineation and differentiation of children with different psychiatric diagnoses, equivalence of sampling procedures across groups, and specification of specific mechanisms by which family relations relate to specific childhood dysfunction.

Experimental Designs

The most rigorous research design examines the relationship between two or more variables by manipulating one or more of the variables, referred to as the independent variable, and observing the effects of the manipulation on other variables, called dependent variables. When appropriate controls are used, the scientist can be reasonably certain that any changes observed in the dependent variables are due to the manipulations of the independent variables.

The following example demonstrates the difference between an experimental and a correlational design. Suppose a scientist wants to examine whether exposure to violence on television results in increased aggression in children. An obvious method would be to obtain a sample of children and then measure (a) the amount of time they spend watching violent television shows and (b) the frequency of aggressive behavior they engage in at home and at school. Calculating the correlation between these two variables would tell the scientist the degree of correlation between these variables. Similarly, the scientist could divide the children into two or three groups based on the amount of television violence they watch, and then test whether these groups of children engage in different rates of aggression. Both of these designs are correlational in that the results will reveal the degree of association between the two variables. However, these designs cannot tell us whether exposure to television violence causes more aggression. A significant correlation, or group differences on aggression, is compatible with at least three interpretations: first, that exposure to television violence causes aggression; second, that aggressive children tend to watch more television violence; or, third, that exposure to television violence and aggression in children are both caused by some third variable such as lack of parental supervision.

By contrast, an experimental design would involve a manipulation of one of the variables. Thus the scientist could randomly assign children to three groups: one group that watches no television, another that watches violence-free television, and a third that watches violent television for a specified period of time. The scientist then has an observer, who is unaware of which group the children belong to, take measures of the level of aggression in each group of children. If the children who watched the violent television evidence more aggression, the experimenter can be reasonably sure that exposure to the television violence caused the aggressive behavior.

There are many ways that experimental designs can be used. Perhaps one of the most important yet neglected experimental designs is the treatment outcome study. An intervention, when carefully specified and controlled, is an independent variable. This design has enormous potential in the child and family psychopathology area. Consider the following example: A clinical psychologist is interested in preventing the development of behavioral problems in children by training parents in skills for child and family management. By carefully manipulating the skills taught to parents and measuring the effects of this training on parenting and child adjustment, the importance of these skills to child adjustment can be evaluated. This form of study is a close approximation of the true experimental study in which an independent variable is manipulated (i.e., the treatment) and its effects on a dependent variable are observed (i.e., the child's adjustment).

If the clinician had taken measures of changes in the family variables that were targeted by the adjunctive intervention (that is, whether the independent variable was properly implemented), more specific conclusions could be made about the effects of those family variables on child development. For example, suppose the clinician had taken measures of parental problem solving and open conflict. If it was found that an improvement in open conflict was the only predictor of improvement in the child's adjustment, we could be reasonably sure that interparental conflict is a key variable predicting positive changes in child adjustment.

In the area of psychotherapy evaluation, hopes were once held that this design could be used to test the relative truth and utility of the different schools of thought. While some researchers argue that these hopes have come to fruition, many disagree, concluding that no differences between the schools of psychotherapy have been demonstrated and that it is pointless to continue looking for them (see Paul, 1986). Consistently, however, this research has focused on general psychotherapeutic approaches with adult disorders, in particular, depression. For example, recent research has failed to find differences between cognitive-behavioral and interpersonal therapies for adult depression.

It seems perfectly understandable that researchers would find little difference between these approaches to the treatment of depression. Psychotherapy with adults is clearly highly dependent upon the therapist-client relationship and the credibility of the therapy, and most differences between therapies will be swamped by similarities in these variables. However, it is a different story when one considers the case of family therapy for childhood disorders. First, while the relationship of the therapist to the family is still important, there is no evidence to indicate, as there is with adult disorders, that this relationship will help the family and the child in and of itself (Kazdin, 1987). Second, it is much more difficult for a family therapy to have effects simply because it is credible to the client. Parents are typically very critical and perhaps even a little cynical when it comes to experts telling them how to manage their child(ren)'s problems. If a child is stealing or lighting fires or fighting, it takes more than a "credible" idea presented to the parents to stop these behaviors.

Third, and perhaps more important, treatment outcome studies in the child and family area do not suffer from one of the most devastating confounds that clouds the adult area. With adults, the independent and dependent variables apply to one person, the client. As therapists, we offer an intervention to the client and then typically ask him or her what effect the intervention has had. This has a number of problems. First, clients like to tell us what they think we want to hear. Second, the therapy often involves interventions that deliberately seek to change the way clients report on their experiences. Thus, even though the client may be behaving or feeling the same, he or she will report differently as a result of therapy. This confound is especially applicable to the purely cognitive therapies.

We often attempt to get over the above problems by conducting independent observations of our adult clients or interviewing others who might have observed the client. However, these procedures are expensive, do not fully overcome the above confounds, and cannot be used with problems that are mostly experiential such as pain, depression, and anxiety. These problems are greatly reduced when we are working with children and families. With many childhood problems, behavioral signs are directly observable by independent observers in clinics, the home, and community settings such as shopping centers (Patterson & Reid, 1984; Sanders, Dadds, et al., 1989). Children are nearly always in the company of adults, either teachers or parents, and thus a range of observers can be sampled regarding the child's behavior.

With family therapy, the independent and dependent variables can be split across individuals. In the case of behavioral family interventions, parents are usually trained in a finite set of skills and the effect on the child is observed. Thus we are looking for a treatment effect in the child, a person whose reporting behaviors we as therapists often have little influence on. Of course, the situation is slightly more complex as the independent variable usually has to be separated into two components.

First, the independent variable is the intervention provided to parents and the dependent variable is the change in the relevant parent behaviors. The latter are then conceptualized as independent to examine any resulting effects on the child. Unfortunately, many studies do not take measures of whether parents implement the intervention but rely solely on changes in child behavior as the dependent outcome measure.

How can child and family treatment outcome studies be designed and implemented so that they really contribute to our basic knowledge of family processes? It will be useful to present some examples of the use of this research logic from our clinic and elsewhere. Very few studies have assessed the effects of marital distress on either adherence to treatment or therapeutic outcome in family therapy. Brody and Forehand (1985) assessed parent and child behavior immediately following a standardized parent training program and found only minimal differences in the outcome for maritally distressed (MD) and nondistressed (ND) mothers of noncompliant children. Dadds, Schwartz, and Sanders (1987) also found no difference between MD and ND parents immediately following treatment. However, the MD group showed significant relapse to baseline levels compared with the ND group at 6 months follow-up to treatment.

Dadds, Sanders, Behrens, and James (1987) observed marital interactions in four MD families containing conduct disordered children throughout their involvement in behavioral family therapy. During pretreatment observations, high rates of parent-parent conflict were observed to co-occur with parent-child conflict. During training in child management skills, the parent-child conflict decreased, but the parent-parent conflict continued concurrently with the reduced incidents of parent-child conflict. Following a brief marital intervention, the marital hostility ceased and remained at low levels through 3-month follow-up. This study suggests an explanation for the poor durability of treatment effects for MD couples observed by Dadds, Sanders, et al. (1987). Behavioral parent training may reduce parent-child conflict but not generalize to other conflict in the family that is functionally related to the former. As time progresses following treatment, the parent-child conflict increases to resume its pretreatment associations with the contextual family distress. In support of this contention, previous data have shown that providing child management training does not necessarily produce reliable increases in marital satisfaction (Griest & Wells, 1983).

Thus these studies show that the role of a complex family variable, in this case marital conflict, can be explored using carefully designed treatment outcome studies. Other examples come from Beach, Sandeen, and O'Leary (1990), who discovered important relationships between adult depression and marital problems with the use of creative treatment outcome studies. Parsons and Alexander (1973) and Alexander and Parsons (1973) similarly used treatment outcome studies to explore the relationship between family communication and delinquency.

To improve the quality of treatment outcome studies, a number of methodological improvements need to be incorporated into treatment outcome research. The first concerns the selection and description of families for whom the treatment is designed. Problems in the family over and above the child's problems should routinely be described with the use of reliable measures. Second, measures need to be taken to validate both the validity and the impact of the intervention (independent variable). Specifically, it needs to be shown that the intervention was delivered as described, that it produced the changes it was intended to produce (e.g., marital communication, problem solving, community contact), and that these changes led to change in parent-child interactions that facilitated improved outcomes for the child. Without these measures of implementation, no conclusion can be made about the specific role of the variable of interest (marital communication, self-control, insularity) in treatment outcome.

Third, new treatments should be compared with the highest quality standard intervention that already exists. It is pointless to show that new interventions produce effects that could have been achieved by providing higher quality or more intensive treatment or simply more of an established treatment. Much research exists to indicate that the effective therapy with parents requires a varied therapy format (direct instructions, therapist modeling, rehearsal and feedback, communication, empathy, and support) that is applied across multiple targets for change in the family (Sanders & James, 1983). Family therapy programs should routinely incorporate these training procedures, especially if they are to be used as control conditions for evaluating the effectiveness of adjunctive techniques or more complex family therapy-type interventions.

There is little point in researchers continuing to compare an active treatment with no treatment. The active treatment will be superior in the vast majority of cases simply because of nonspecific treatment effects. Treatment outcome studies should be designed to allow maximum inference about causal variables in the child and family. Factorial designs that cross intervention type with risk factor type allow these conclusions.

SUMMARY

A variety of research designs can be used in the evaluation of the role of the family in child behavioral disturbance. However, only rarely have these designs been used to their full potential in this area and a number of design improvements should be considered by researchers in the future. These include the use of independent data sources, multivariate models in correlational designs, appropriate control groups, and treatment outcome studies that are conceptualized as experimental manipulations of theoretically important variables. In the next chapter, substantive findings about the role of the family in child behavioral disturbance will be reviewed with respect to variations in research design logic.

7

SPECIFIC
RESEARCH FINDINGS

In this chapter, we review substantive findings concerning the role of family variables in the development, maintenance, and treatment of four common types of child disturbance: depression, conduct problems, anxiety, and somatic complaints using the example of recurrent abdominal pain. All of these are relatively common and disabling conditions for which a range of research methodologies have been employed: (a) case studies, (b) correlational studies and group comparison designs, and (c) experimental designs including treatment outcome and longitudinal studies.

CHILDHOOD DEPRESSION

A number of case studies of depressed children and their families have been published and a number of common themes emerge (Sines, 1987). Specifically, these families are typically described as characterized by loss and separation, parental depression and other psychological disorders, marital conflict and separation, parental rejection, and aggression toward the child (Connell, 1972; Cytryn & McKnew, 1974).

Correlational designs have examined correlations between reports of depression in children and various family factors in nonclinical children. Significant correlations with childhood depression have been found in these populations for low SES (Mullins, Siegel, & Hodges, 1985), marital discord (Emery, 1982), parental depression (Downey & Coyne, 1990), lack of parental care and nurturance, and parental rejection (Crook, Riskin, Eliot, 1981; Lefkowitz & Tesiny, 1985). It should be noted that in many of these studies depression refers to a score on a checklist rather than a clinically diagnosable condition, and typically the scores would cover the low end of the range of scores. Furthermore, these correlations are usually significant statistically but very small, accounting for little of the variance in depression scores (Sines, 1987). Published failures to find correlations exist for a number of family factors, especially when depression in girls is considered (Sines, 1987), highlighting the need to consider the child's gender when relating childhood behavioral disturbance to family environment.

Group comparison designs have demonstrated that depressed children differ from nonclinical children on the following factors: depressive cognitive style in the child (Kazdin, 1990), family interaction and reinforcement style promoting depressed behaviors (Cole & Rehm, 1986; Dadds et al., 1992; Sanders et al., 1992), more conflict in the family (Forehand et al., 1988; Stark, Humphrey, Crook, & Lewis, 1990), and less of an outward social recreational style (Stark et al., 1990).

Families of depressed children do not consistently have higher levels of marital discord. Sanders et al. (1992) found no evidence of marital problems in a mixed sample of depressed 7- to 14-year-olds; however, Puig-Antich et al. (1993) found severe marital difficulties in the parents of adolescents with major depressive disorders. Differences could be due to the age of the children, the severity of the depression, and differences in reporting source (in the Sanders et al., 1992, study, parents reported on their relationship but reports came from the depressed adolescents in the Puig-Antich et al., 1993, study). Additional research is needed to clarify this area; however, the review by Sines (1987) concluded that marital discord is found equally in other clinical and nonclinical children. Thus it is unlikely that marital discord is a specific risk factor for depression in children.

Furthermore, a recent study (Green, Loeber, & Lahey, 1992) found no evidence that depression in children is associated with deviant family hierarchies (Haley, 1976; Minuchin, 1974) in which the child exercises more power in the family than the parents.

Thus the group comparison studies lead to the conclusion that the variables that consistently discriminate childhood depression are the cognitive style of the child, the amount of depression and conflict in the family, and family interaction patterns that promote and support the child's depressive symptomatology. In the first instance, depressed children appear to share the sort of cognitive biases that have repeatedly been shown to characterize depressed adults. That is, they are more likely than their peers to attend to pessimistic aspects of external and internal stimuli (Brewin, 1987). With respect to family interactions, Cole and Rehm (1986) showed that parents of depressed children are more likely to give attention to the child contingent upon failure, and are more likely to ignore success. Similarly, Dadds et al. (1992) examined differences in family interaction, observed in the home, between conduct disorder (CD), depressed, mixed depressed and conduct disordered, and comparison children and their families. The results indicated that differences in family interaction patterns could be detected across the diagnostic groups. In a related study, Sanders et al. (1992) showed that clinic-based problem-solving discussion revealed differences in the behavior of CD, depressed, mixed, and comparison children and their mothers.

The results of the Cole and Rehm (1986), Dadds et al. (1992), and Sanders et al. (1992) studies provide some of the first evidence that family interaction patterns, observed in the home or clinic, might discriminate between different forms of child psychopathology, that is, depression and conduct disorder. It should be noted that the Cole and Rehm (1986), the Sanders et al. (1992), and the Dadds et al. (1992) studies used both nonclinical and clinical nondepressed children as control groups and so their findings appear to be specific to depression in children rather than to clinic-referred children in general.

Treatment outcome studies with depressed children and adolescents are rare. A number of studies have shown that cognitive-behavioral interventions can decrease depression in children (Kazdin, 1990); however, no published studies are available to show that changes in family process or structure, due either to intervention or to natural change, can lead to changes in levels of child depression.

In conclusion, we find that family factors that are argued to be associated with childhood depression vary according to the methodologies used to assess them. Case studies point to a range of factors; however, there is little hard evidence to support many of these and the support becomes more scarce as we examine the more rigorous experimental designs. Strong evidence is found for depression in the family (although not clearly more than clinical, nondepressed children) and for cognitive characteristics of the children themselves. Mixed evidence is found for marital problems in parents. A few well-controlled studies have shown that family interactions may differentiate families of depressed children from other families but these data are limited to family interactions directly associated with the display of depressive behaviors by the child. Some self-report evidence exists that families of depressed children are more conflictual, enmeshed, and less sociable than nonclinical children.

CONDUCT PROBLEMS

Of all the childhood disorders, conduct problems in children have received the most extensive study from researchers and clinicians (Kazdin, 1987). They often begin as oppositional behavior in early childhood and, in their most severe form, progress into recurrent antisocial and aggressive behavior in the teen years and into personal and occupational disruption in adulthood (Kazdin, 1987). The role of the family appears to be particularly important in the early years (Patterson, 1982, 1986).

Case studies have been fairly consistent in describing the families of these children as aggressive, disorganized, and chaotic; economically stressed; marked by parental rejection, harsh discipline, and abuse; and disrupted by divorce and separation (Kazdin, 1987). At the systemic level, there have been a number of case descriptions that describe these families as marked by chaotic, disengaged relationships and as having power imbalances (e.g., Minuchin, 1967).

Correlational studies have tended to confirm this pattern of aggression and disruption. Group comparison studies have confirmed a pattern in which a range of risk factors are associated with increased risk for aggression and conduct problems. These include marital distress, parental depression, paternal antisocial problems, socioeconomic stress and social isolation, harsh punishment, insufficient parental monitoring, abuse, and neglect (Hetherington & Martin, 1979; Kazdin, 1987). Perhaps one of the reasons for this plethora of risk factors is that conduct problems are such a diverse group of behaviors that, in a categorical sense, are comorbid with so many other forms of child disturbance. Conduct problems are found in approximately 70% of children with *any* psychiatric diagnosis (Rutter, Cox, Tupling, Berger, & Yule, 1975) and many different forms of child psychopathology contain similar discrete behavior problems. For example, aggression is commonly associated with conduct disorders and attention deficit disorder with hyperactivity, some forms of developmental delay, adjustment disorders, and depression (Kazdin, 1987).

The case studies and correlational designs referred to above leave little doubt that these associations exist between conduct problems and a range of family factors. Studies demonstrating that experimental manipulations of parent behavior result in concomitant changes in aggressive, noncompliant child behaviors have been common in the child behavior therapy literature (Lochman, 1990). The most important parenting behaviors are use of harsh discipline, lack of modeling and positive attention to prosocial behavior, and deficits in monitoring of the child's activities

(Loeber, 1990; Patterson, 1986). These clinical trials have typically involved the modification of parent behavior via parent training programs and behavioral family therapy (Miller & Prinz, 1990) and have provided strong evidence of the dependent relationship between oppositional child behavior and interactional patterns with parents. Specifically, these interactional patterns involve the direct contingencies that parents provide to aggressive and oppositional child behavior.

It appears that disturbed children tend to come from families who engage in relatively high rates of the disturbed behavior themselves in their day-to-day interactions. The aggressive child is regularly exposed to conflicts among family members, is likely to receive high rates of aversive instructions, and many of his or her behaviors will be followed by aversive consequences regardless of their appropriateness.

There is also evidence to support the systemic hypothesis that children with conduct problems come from families with deviant or reversed family hierarchies in which the child has more power than the parents (Haley, 1976; Minuchin, 1974). Green et al. (1992) showed that these structures appear to be specific to families of children with conduct disorder (compared with overanxious, oppositional disorder, depression, and attention deficit-hyperactivity). However, examination of their longitudinal data revealed that conduct disorder in the child predicted a deviant family hierarchy 1 year later, but the reverse was not true. Thus it appears that the family system organizes itself into this reversed hierarchical form because of the child's aggressive behavior, and is not a causal factor.

Treatment studies clearly support the role of family interaction patterns in the development of conduct problems in children; that is, modifying the balance between parental attention to prosocial child behavior and parental attention to problematic child behavior results in reliable decreases in conduct problems in children (Kazdin, 1987; Lochman, 1990). A number of treatment studies have also shown that modifying personal distress, problem solving and communication skills, and marital discord in parents is also associated with reductions in conduct problems in children (Miller & Prinz, 1990). However, it should be noted that these studies have modified these parental factors in conjunction with a program that trains parents in child management skills. It is unlikely that modification of the parental factor would lead to direct changes in the child's adjustment without the parallel change in child-rearing techniques. This has led authors to argue that these broader family issues affect the child via their impact on the parent's ability to implement positive child management skills (Dadds, 1987). Studies are not available in the literature that show that a change in parental distress and marital discord alone—that is, without associated changes in parenting skills—results in improvements in child behavior. Similarly, controlled studies are not available that show that a change in systemic aspects of family process results in improvements in child behavior.

ANXIETY

Case studies of anxious children and their families tend to describe the families as marked by anxiety and marked by enmeshed and highly structured family systems. In research up until the 1970s reviewed by Hetherington and Martin (1979), the mother of anxious children is consistently described as domineering, overprotective, and overinvolved with the child. However, as Hetherington and Martin (1979) point out, this image of the overprotective mother and the highly structured family system is based on "rather indirect sources of data" (p. 61).

Correlational studies are far more limited in the support they provide for family factors. Support can be found for the presence of elevated levels of anxiety in the parents of anxious children (e.g., Bernstein & Borchardt, 1991). Marital conflict also correlates with parental reports of anxiety in nonclinical children (Dadds & Powell, 1991); however, group comparisons show that parents of clinically diagnosed anxious children do not have more distressed marriages than other clinic-referred and nonreferred children (Dadds, Barrett, Rapee, & Ryan, 1993). The Dadds et al. data also used the FACES scale, and no support was found for the idea that families of anxious children have different levels of adaptability and cohesion than other nonclinical families. Furthermore, Green et al. (1992) found no evidence for the presence of deviant family hierarchies, as predicted by family systems theory (Haley, 1976; Minuchin, 1974), in the families of overanxious boys. However, a study by Stark et al. (1990) showed that anxious children saw their families as less supportive, less sociable, more conflictual, and more enmeshed than nonclinical children. However, the results were even more striking for depressed and mixed depressed-anxious children and so these factors are unlikely to be specific correlates of childhood anxiety.

A recent study has indicated that parents of anxious children may differ from other parents in terms of the way they teach their children to interpret and respond to ambiguous threat cues. Dadds et al. (1993) showed that parents of anxious children were more likely to encourage the anxious child to make threatening interpretations of, and thus choose avoidant responses to, ambiguous social situations, compared with parents of non-clinical and aggressive children.

Experimental studies with anxious children are quite limited. A number of single case experimental designs have shown that changes in parental attention can result in decreases in child anxiety. For example, Heard, Dadds, and Conrad (1992) showed that changes in parental attention were successful in reducing fears of the dark and of medical procedures in three children, and that these improvements were not associated with any broader changes in the marital relationship or the family environment. Thus direct modification of childhood fear appears to be possible via the modification of parental attention to that fear, without causing compensatory problems elsewhere in the family system.

Controlled treatment studies have shown that two factors are reliably related to changes in child anxiety: child exposure to the fearful stimuli with associated cognitive work and family behaviors directly focused on the display of anxiety in the family. First, a number of trials have shown that helping anxious children face the stimuli they are afraid of helps decrease the level of fear (Dadds et al., 1991). Many of these studies also involve a cognitive component in which the child is taught to process information about threat in a more constructive way. For example, in the Kendall cognitive-behavioral model, the child is taught to relax his or her body, expect good things to happen, and reinforce him- or herself for coping with feared events.

Only one controlled treatment study has evaluated the role of family variables in the remediation of child anxiety. Barrett, Dadds, Rapee, and Ryan (1993) treated a large group of anxious children (overanxious, avoidant, and with separation anxiety) who were randomly assigned to either a cognitive-behavioral treatment based on Kendall's model or the same CBT model plus a family intervention that ran in parallel over a 14-week period. The family intervention involved three phases: (a) parent skills for managing child distress and avoidance, (b) parent skills for managing their own anxiety, and (c) parental communication and problem-solving skills.

Evaluation of the program at the end of treatment revealed that 61% of children in the CBT group no longer met a *DSM-III-R* diagnosis, compared with 88% in the combined treatment, and less than 30% in the wait-list control group. At 12 months follow-up, the relative superiority of the CBT plus family condition was maintained.

The Barrett study also examined whether the CBT plus family intervention changed the way parents of anxious children taught their children to interpret and respond to threat. As discussed above, these parents were found to ask more questions of their children and reinforce more avoidance in their children when faced with an ambiguous threat situation than were parents of nonclinical and clinical nonanxious children. At the end of treatment, this tendency had greatly diminished. That is, after treatment, parents of anxious children were no longer focusing so much of their child's attention onto threat and avoidance strategies. Thus it appears that this mechanism may be an important factor in the development and treatment of these disorders.

Thus it can be seen that the variables that emerge from research so far as being reliably associated with anxiety in children differ according to the methodology used. Those factors that appear to be robust across designs are elevated levels of anxiety in parents and the way parents of anxious children focus the child's attention onto threat and reinforce the child for avoidance. Little evidence is available to support disturbance in the families of anxious children at the systemic level.

SOMATIC COMPLAINTS

One of the most common forms of somatic complaint that comes to the attention of mental health services is functional recurrent abdominal pain (RAP). About 10% of schoolchildren report the problem and it is slightly more common in males (Apley, 1975). To warrant a clinical diagnosis, the pain must be severe enough to interfere with regular activities, have occurred at least twice before, and not be attributable to a detectable physical illness.

Reports of the families of these children typically point to the presence of the following factors: family history of somatic complaints, recent loss of a relationship with family or friend, overprotective or domineering parent(s), marital or family conflict, extreme life changes, and high family pressure for achievement (Sines, 1987). However, the review by Sines (1987) concluded that none of the studies contributing to this picture were designed well enough to warrant the conclusion that any of these variables is a specific risk factor for RAP. That is, when non-RAP clinically referred children are used as controls, the presence of these risk factors does not differ across groups.

Very few researchers have attempted to modify RAP in children by changing family process. However, there is one noteworthy exception. Sanders, Rebgetz, et al. (1989) assessed a behavioral family intervention for children who had RAP. The intervention involved training parents to reinforce the child for pain-free periods, to decrease attention to pain behavior, and to discourage avoidance behavior in the child. The results indicated that the intervention produced significant decreases in the frequency of child pain behaviors compared with a control condition in which matched RAP children and their families received standard pediatric care. The majority of family intervention children reported they were no longer experiencing pain after the intervention.

Sanders, Rebgetz, et al. (1990), in a related paper, were also interested in examining changes in the family system throughout the intervention. They reasoned that, if the child's pain was functionally related to a disturbed family system, then producing changes in the child's pain by way of changes in parental contingencies applied to the child's behavior should be accompanied by changes in the family process. To test this, they analyzed data on the family before and after the family intervention. No changes were found on the Family Environment Scale (Moos, 1974) completed by parents and children separately, on a measure of marital problems, or on measures of child behavior problems.

Thus it appears that no change in the family system occurred in response to the change in the child's pain, apart from the change in parental management of the pain that was specifically targeted by the intervention. These results support the conclusion that functional childhood pain is at least in part maintained by the reactions it produces in parents but is unlikely to be associated with broader aspects of family functioning.

In conclusion, a number of family factors have been related to the development of childhood RAP on the basis of clinical observation and correlational studies. When psychiatric controls are used in comparison studies, none of these factors appears to differentiate the families of RAP children from other children. The experimental study by Sanders, Rebgetz, et al. (1989, 1990) indicates that RAP is functionally related to the reactions it produces in parents but is not related to other areas of family functioning such as those dimensions of the family measured by the FES, marital problems, and other behavior problems in the child.

Other psychosomatic complaints in children are hypothesized to be related to family environment. Hetherington and Martin (1979) reviewed research into family factors associated with childhood asthma. Again, a consistent image of the mother-child relationship is portrayed in this literature as overly enmeshed and "symbiotic," with the mother being highly dominating toward a dependent and submissive child. Most of the evidence contributing to this picture is, however, based on clinical impressions and self-reports taken after the asthma has reached clinical severity rather than on objective measures of family and parent-child interaction.

There is one study, however, that is notable for the unusual experimental design it employed. Purcell et al. (1969) divided 60 asthmatic children into two groups on the basis of parental reports of how important emotional reactions were to the onset of asthma attacks. As part of the experimental design, families moved out of the home for a 2-week period and the asthmatic child remained there in the care of another surrogate mother. Results indicated that significant improvement in respiratory functioning occurred during separation only for the group of children for whom emotional factors were thought to be a significant antecedent to attacks. The mechanisms of influence are not clear; however, this experimental manipulation appears to indicate that the presence of family members is associated with occurrence of asthma attacks. A multitude of explanations could be invoked that do not, however, necessarily implicate the role of the family system in the development or maintenance of childhood asthma.

Another psychosomatic complaint that is frequently argued to be associated with a disturbed family system is anorexia nervosa. Most contemporary researchers point to the multidimensional causes of this problem (e.g., Garfinkel & Garner, 1982); however, some notable clinical theorists have argued that this problem is primarily an expression of family dysfunction. Crisp (1980) and Bruch (1973) argued that anorexia nervosa is characterized by a fear of facing the interpersonal and sexual maturity demands that come with adolescence and adulthood. Thus the anorexic stops eating to reverse growth toward maturity and independence. This process is seen as being functionally related to a disturbed family system in that the eating problem satisfies a number of unresolved family issues about independence and emotional expression.

Family systems theorists have placed more emphasis on the role of the family. Selvini-Palazzoli (1974) and Minuchin, Rosman, and Baker (1978) emphasize two key factors: (a) a disturbed family system usually marked by unexpressed marital conflict, enmeshment, rigidity, and inability to problem solve and (b) the involvement of the child (and his or her eating problem) in the parental conflict. Some studies have provided indirect support for the role of this interdependence of the child's and the parent's problems in anorexia. For example, Crisp, Harding, and McGuiness (1974) showed that parents of anorexic girls tended to display more neurotic disturbance after their daughters' weight had been restored via an inpatient program. Humphrey (1989) was able to discriminate between families of anorexic, bulimic, and nonclinical patients on the basis of direct observations of family interaction. However, this evidence only indirectly supports a systemic model of eating disorder, and other attempts to find evidence to support these family models have generally failed (Palmer, Marshall, & Oppenheimer, 1987; Ratsam & Gillberg, 1991; Steiger, Liquornik, Chapman, & Hussain, 1991).

A recent study assessed the influence of family interaction on treatment outcome for anorexia. Le Grange, Eisler, Dare, and Hodes (1992) showed that anorexics who made poor progress came from families who were significantly more critical than those who made good progress at 6 months follow-up. This indicates that family style may have an impact on prognosis in anorexia. However, the impact of criticism on poor therapy outcome is not unique to anorexia and, in general, research has shown that high levels of criticism are not a feature of families with an anorexic member (Goldstein, 1981).

SUMMARY

There are four consistent findings that emerge from the above review regardless of what particular childhood disorder is being considered. First, the importance of various family factors for various childhood disorders varies according to the methodology used to assess them. Case studies consistently point to a host of family factors that research using more rigorous experimental designs fails to support. Clinical descriptions are an important source of theories and hypotheses about the nature and causes of psychopathology, but it is clear that, without submitting their speculations to carefully controlled research, they are likely to be inaccurate in the models of family influence they contribute.

Second, based on clinical observations and some comparison studies in which the specific clinical group is compared with nonclinical controls, a number of family characteristics have been hypothesized to be related to the onset of almost every form of psychopathology in children. Perhaps the most commonly mentioned of these are marital problems and family conflict. When appropriate clinical control groups are used, however, the specific association of these factors to any particular form of child psychopathology is lost. That is, these factors appear to operate as a general risk factor for behavioral problems rather than a specific causal variable.

Third, despite the predictions of psychodynamic and family systems theorists, treatment programs in which the child's problematic behavior is directly modified are not typically associated with compensatory

changes in the marital and family system. This has been clearly demonstrated for childhood conduct disorder, anxiety, and somatic complaints.
The one study that showed an increase in parental neurosis following
restoration of normal weight in their adolescent daughters (Crisp et al.,
1974) was confounded by other changes. For example, restoration in weight
was also associated with the daughters returning home; having an adolescent come home could be distressing to parents regardless of the anorexia.
Thus there is little support for the notion that a child's symptoms serve to
protect other conflicts in the family from being expressed and that direct
modification of the child's symptoms will cause deterioration in other
parts of the family.

The fourth point also concerns the type of family processes that are
uniquely associated with specific types of childhood disturbance. The
evidence reviewed above shows that family processes that are closely
linked to the specific behavioral problems of the child appear to be far
more important than more general aspects of the family's style. For each
of the disorders reviewed, evidence was clearly supportive of a model in
which parents appear to model, prompt, and provide contingent attention
to the particular behavioral problem the child has. Parents of aggressive
children reward aggression and ignore prosocial behavior; parents of
depressed children appear to reward self-denigration and model a depressive cognitive style; parents of anxious children appear to model fear and
avoidance and reward caution. This is not to say that parents are causing
the child's problem, especially not intentionally. Rather, it appears that
parents become trapped into a cycle with the child in which the behavioral
problem becomes an important, if not dominating, focus for the way in
which the family interacts.

However, there is little evidence that broader aspects of the family such
as cohesiveness, adaptability, power imbalances, alliances, double binds,
and other systemic concepts are reliably associated with specific forms of
child psychopathology. In some cases, this is because the appropriate
research has not been done. In other cases, the research has been done but
the results have not supported the importance of these characteristics. A
good example comes again from the association of marital and childhood
problems. A wealth of research has shown that self-report measures of marital
adjustment are correlated with reports of childhood behavior problems
(Emery, 1982; Grych & Fincham, 1990). The more the measures of marital
adjustment focus on global aspects of marital satisfaction, the weaker the
correlation with child problems; conversely, the more the marital measure
focuses on open hostility associated with child-rearing tasks, the stronger

the correlation with child problems. Thus this evidence shows again that, the closer the measure of family functioning is to the child's particular problems, the stronger the relationship. The more one moves to more global measures of the family system, the less important the factor appears to be for the child's adjustment. This is contrary to systemic concepts of homeostasis in which the child's problem is taken as being a symptom of a more hidden, amorphous problem such as repressed marital dissatisfaction (e.g., Framo, 1975).

8

FAMILY THERAPY

WHAT IS FAMILY THERAPY?

Family therapy is not a homogeneous approach. Clearly the integrating theme is that an intervention is aimed at changing the way a family functions to alleviate the emotional and behavioral problems of constituent members, relational problems between members, and problems with the interactions the family has with its social and cultural context. But family therapy can take many different forms, varying in theoretical premises, targets for change, and the procedures used.

A recent review in the *Annual Review of Psychology* shows that even the basic assumption that family therapy is about changing families is problematic. Bednar, Burlingame, and Masters (1988) argued that what is called family therapy is often no more than individual therapy provided in the context of more than one family member being present. Furthermore, because family therapy is often assumed to be about changing aspects of the family as a whole, many intervention types that probably should be regarded as "family therapy" are often not discussed. For example, in reviews of the efficacy of family therapy, interventions in which parents are trained in management strategies to reduce conduct problems in offspring are usually not included (e.g., Kaslow, 1987). On the contrary, marital therapy is usually included in reviews of family therapy and many of the conclusions regarding the process and efficacy of family therapy are based substantially on research into dyadic marital therapy (e.g., see Gurman, Kniskern, & Pinsof, 1986).

Clearly, a definition that includes any intervention in which more than one family member is part of the consultation process would be overly inclusive and would add to confusion in reviews of family therapy. However, to derive an accurate picture of the usefulness of family therapy, these parent training-type interventions should be included. For the purposes of this review, family therapy will be defined as any psychosocial intervention in which human distress is targeted for amelioration by consulting with and producing change in the way two or more family members interact with each other or their social context. Given the current focus on children in the family, the present review will not cover dyadic marital therapies in a comprehensive way.

DOES FAMILY THERAPY WORK?

Reviews by Gurman et al. (1986) and Hazelrigg, Cooper, and Borduin (1987) have shown that families who received family therapy showed improvement relative to families who were assigned to wait-list conditions. However, both these reviews pointed to the poor quality of research that has characterized these intervention studies, and thus concluded that their conclusions were encouraging but tentative. Hazelrigg et al. (1987) made their conclusions based on 20 studies that met certain criteria for methodological rigor. These outcome studies included a mix of structural, strategic, and behavioral interventions (no studies of systemic family intervention met the inclusion criteria). In the review by Bednar et al. (1988), the authors differentiated between systemic (strategic, structural, and systemic) and behavioral approaches. With regard to systemic approaches, their conclusions were very critical of the idea that these interventions actually achieve change by the theoretical mechanisms that their theoretical bases prescribe. That is, the outcome studies did not measure the theoretical constructs that were hypothesized to be critical to change in the family. Thus Bednar et al. (1988) argue that there is no evidence that these models of therapy actually modify the family system at all; rather, when change occurs, it probably does so due to mechanisms of change that are common to all "good" psychotherapy, that is, a positive relationship with clients, opportunity for problem solving, ventilation of emotion, and formulation of plans for change.

Bednar et al. (1988) argued that the behavioral family therapies are not subject to this criticism. Evaluation studies of behavioral family intervention have typically taken measures of family processes that are hypothesized to be important in the maintenance of the particular problem, and researchers have been able to show that change in these family processes is associated with improvement in the referred problem (see Sanders & Dadds, 1993).

One of the best examples of an intervention trial for family therapy was conducted by Parsons and Alexander (1973; see also Alexander & Parsons, 1973). Their intervention incorporated a combination of behavioral (parent training for managing disruptive, aggressive behavior) and family problem-solving and communication strategies, and their clients were families of delinquent and aggressive youth. The intervention was successful in reducing the problematic youth behavior compared with individual psychotherapy, as we would expect, but the methodological characteristics of the study make the trial an important contribution. Outcome measures included both self-report and observational measures collected from a variety of independent sources. A number of these measures were specifically aimed at measuring the intervention targets (parenting behavior, family communication, and problem solving), thus the authors were able to make specific conclusions about the mechanisms of change in the families.

Comparisons between different types of family therapy can be made by examining the evidence in support of the treatment compared with no treatment controls as well as by examining studies that directly compare different types of family therapy with each other. Only a handful of studies have done this, but the quality of these studies tends to be relatively high. Robin (1981) compared a "behavioral-systems" family therapy for parent-adolescent conflict with alternative treatments that included a mix of systemic, eclectic, and psychodynamic family therapies. The outcome measures included a mix of self-report and observational measures. Both groups showed reductions in parent-adolescent conflict immediately posttreatment on the self-report measures. However, the behavioral-systems group showed superior outcome on the measures of problem solving, communication, and self-reported satisfaction with therapy.

Szykula, Morris, Sudweeks, and Saygar (1987) compared the effectiveness of strategic and behavioral family therapy for a mixed sample of behaviorally and emotionally disturbed children and their families. Only self-report measures were used to evaluate treatment. A t-test comparison showed that the outcome was similar and positive for both therapy groups. However, an analysis of outcome by severity of presenting problem showed that families with the more severe problems responded more favorably to the behavioral intervention.

Wells and Egan (1988) compared behavioral family therapy with systems family therapy in the treatment of child oppositional disorder. Their study was well controlled in that it employed a crossover design that controlled for therapist effects. Advanced clinical students undertaking courses in systemic and behavioral family interventions were assigned to referred families while undertaking each course and were supervised by the teaching staff in each of the courses. The results showed no differences between the two therapies on measures of parental emotional and marital adjustment; parents in both groups showed a decrease in anxiety and depression. Direct observations of the family, however, showed that the behavioral intervention was superior in producing improvements in parental positive attention and child compliance (the presenting problem).

Barkley, Guevremont, Anastopoulos, and Fletcher (1992) compared structural family therapy, behavioral parent training, and problem-solving and communication training in the treatment of adolescents with attention deficit-hyperactivity problems. Many of the children also had oppositional behavior problems. Dependent measures were both self-report and observational. Parents were equally and highly satisfied with all three treatments, and all three treatments were associated with improvements in parent-adolescent conflict and communication as well as personal adjustment of the adolescent at home and at school. Finally, Brunk, Henggeler, and Whelan (1987) compared behavioral parent training presented in a group format to parents with an individualized systems intervention for parents at risk for child abuse and neglect. The latter intervention included individualized behavioral parent training given in the home, counseling, interpersonal problem solving, and a host of other interventions tailored to the individual needs of the parent. As expected, both interventions produced positive changes but the individualized multisystemic therapy produced a better outcome on a subset of the observational measures.

WHAT TREATMENT
FOR WHAT DISORDER?

The most sophisticated and practically useful question we can ask relates to what type of family therapy has been shown to be effective for what type of problem treated with what population in what setting. The level of research sophistication in family therapy is still quite basic and so questions relating to setting and populations are far from being adequately addressed. However, a number of conclusions can be made about the efficacy of different family therapies for different childhood disorders.

The most thoroughly researched treatment has been behavioral family therapy for childhood conduct problems. Over the last few decades, a sophisticated technology for treating aggressive and conduct problem children has developed with a firm empirical base (Kazdin, 1987; Lochman, 1990; Miller & Prinz, 1990; Sanders & Dadds, 1993). The core of this approach is training parents to apply learning principles to the child's behavior. Usually, the parents are trained in reinforcement strategies for promoting prosocial behaviors, and extinction and punishment strategies for reducing aggressive and oppositional behaviors. This core strategy is usually embedded in a supportive relationship between therapist and the family, and the specific reinforcement and punishment strategies are supplemented with other strategies needed by each individual family. These might include planned activities training for encouraging independent prosocial child behavior, family communication and problem-solving skills, anger and depression management skills, or marital communication. These supplementary interventions have been reviewed recently by Miller and Prinz (1990).

Research evaluating the use of behavioral family interventions for child conduct problems has supported the efficacy of this approach in the short term and over follow-up periods up to years after the termination of treatment. The field has been reasonably responsive to the data that have emerged on the strengths and limitations of interventions. For example, research suggesting that some parents have difficulties in generalizing their parenting skills across settings or over time led to several studies designed to promote better generalization and maintenance effects (e.g., Forehand & Atkeson, 1977; Koegel, Glahn, & Nieminen, 1978; Sanders & Glynn, 1981). Research has shown that parents undergoing behavioral parent training are also generally satisfied consumers and view the specific behavioral techniques (e.g., praise, time-out) taught in these training programs as both effective and acceptable (McMahon & Forehand, 1983; Webster-Stratton, 1989). Much less is known about how children view the treatment process although Dadds, Adlington, and Christensen (1987) found that both nonclinical and oppositional children rated time-out as an acceptable strategy for parents to use. Furey and Basili (1988) found that the child's level of deviant behavior was unrelated to parental consumer satisfaction but having a noncompliant daughter, low SES, depression, and poor parenting skills were all predictors of dissatisfaction.

As the field of behavioral parent training has matured, both empirical evidence and clinical experience have suggested that not all parents or families benefit to the same extent from treatment (Miller & Prinz, 1990), and difficulties are commonly encountered when there are concurrent marital problems, parental depression, and other family difficulties such as economic hardship. Several authors have made various proposals to improve the outcome of treatment by expanding the focus of treatment (Miller & Prinz, 1990; Wahler, 1980). These suggestions have included providing additional skills training to overcome problems that are hypothesized to be related to their child management difficulties. Such adjunctive interventions include teaching parents self-management skills (Griest et al., 1982), providing concurrent marital therapy (Dadds, Adlington, & Christensen, 1987), providing training in the selection and arrangement of activities for children in high-risk situations (Sanders & Christensen, 1985; Sanders & Dadds, 1982), providing anger management training (Goldstein, Keller, & Erne, 1985), providing social support training (Dadds & McHugh, 1992), and developing better home-school liaison for the management of school-based behavioral problems (Blechman, 1984).

While each of these suggestions has merits with selected cases, efficiency dictates that it is better to include only those components that are required to achieve the therapeutic objectives negotiated with a family. One of the challenges facing behavioral family therapy over the next few decades is to develop models of family process and intervention that are not so piecemeal but that flow from a more integrated model of the family.

The next best area of evaluation of family therapy is with parent-adolescent conflict. Studies such as those by Robin (1981) and Alexander and Parsons (1973) have shown that combinations of behavioral parent training and family communication and problem-solving training are effective in ameliorating these problems in the majority of cases. Educative interventions of this type have also been shown to be effective with families in which a member has a diagnosed psychotic disorder. Falloon et al. (1985) have shown that psychoeducational family interventions are effective in reducing the return of psychotic symptoms and subsequent hospitalization in such cases.

It is also possible to draw some conclusions about problems that have not been shown to be helped by family therapy. For example, no evidence is available to show that the Milan or strategic approach to family therapy is effective in treating schizophrenia. Similarly, no evidence is available to support the efficacy of any form of family therapy with anorexia and bulimia, childhood depression, and autism, although case studies are available to indicate that family therapy approaches may have potential. In many cases, the necessary research simply hasn't been done.

Another important issue concerns the observation that family therapy can be associated with deterioration in child and family functioning. For example, Terkelson (1983) showed that using a systemic family therapy approach during intake assessment can be associated with an increase in family distress and disturbance. Similarly, Gurman et al. (1986) argued that certain characteristics of therapists may be reliably associated with deterioration in the family. These include providing little structure within sessions and using a highly confrontational approach with sensitive emotional material. Conversely, therapists who promote family interaction, and give support and structure, were seen as minimizing these problems.

These process problems have been discussed by Becvar and Becvar (1993) with reference to the underlying assumptions of particular family therapies and epistemologies. They argue that, in keeping with a systemic causal philosophy, families will tend to adopt the framework of the therapist; even observation is a process that changes the observed party. Thus family therapists and researchers alike must be aware that they cannot adopt the role of objective observer, observing a separate system that has a reality unrelated to the observation system. The adoption of an assessment and intervention strategy is in and of itself a value-ridden behavior that influences its subject matter.

The growing awareness of the interdependency of the mental health systems and the families and children they seek to assess and help has led a number of authors to talk about a new and growing alliance with families (e.g., Orford, 1987) in which professionals and families interact in a "teamwork" approach to mental health problems (Dadds, 1989; Sanders & Dadds, 1993).

Some other general and important conclusions about the process and outcome of family therapy have been made by Becvar and Becvar (1993), Bednar et al., (1988), Gurman et al. (1986), Hazelrigg et al. (1987), Piercy and Sprenkle (1990), and Sanders and Dadds (1993). These include the following:

1. When successful treatment outcome is achieved, it usually occurs within (approximately) 1 to 20 sessions. No evidence is available to support longer, protracted therapies.

2. Using more than one therapist, or a team of therapists observing from behind two-way mirrors, has not been shown to be more effective than using one therapist.

3. The same therapist relationship building skills that have been shown to be effective in individual therapy (e.g., empathy, listening, problem solving, structuring) are also associated with positive processes and outcomes in family therapy.

4. The adoption of one narrow school of thought or therapy technique is not associated with improved outcomes. Therapies that combine multiple levels of assessment and intervention are emerging as the most successful.

A CRITIQUE OF FAMILY THERAPY OUTCOME RESEARCH

Reviews of family therapy research have been unanimous in their concern over the lack of quality characterizing the field. Although there has been some improvement, it is worth reiterating the major design considerations here. (a) The underlying philosophy of the therapy should be operationalized into concrete procedural terms. Treatment strategies should be described in specific detail to allow for replication. Therapists don't always follow prescribed treatment protocols and thus checks need to be made that the therapy is presented as described. (b) Single assessment strategies, or assessments based entirely on one mode (e.g., self report), are not sufficient. Multiple assessment strategies should be employed that sample phenomena across varying levels of individual and family functioning and as reported by various observers both within and external to the family. (c) Assessment strategies should include measure(s) that clearly operationalize the underlying philosophy of the therapy. Thus, if the clinician hypothesizes that parental attention is maintaining childhood aggression, a measure of amount of attention to aggressive versus nonaggressive behaviors should be incorporated. If the clinician hypothesizes that the child's problem is a scapegoat system of a dysfunctional marriage, a measure of marital functioning should be included to test this mechanism. (d) Adequate control groups need to be carefully selected. Given the state of the art, the use of wait-list controls should be limited to problems for which no effective treatment has been demonstrated. For all other problems, a state-of-the-art control group should be employed. (e) Outcome should be assessed in terms of consumer acceptability and satisfaction, and resource usage (i.e., therapist hours, clinic facilities), as well as traditional measures of functioning; and outcome measures should be analyzed in terms of clinical significance as well as statistical significance (see Kendall, 1991). (f) Client populations should be described in adequate detail and on well-recognized criteria to allow comparison with other studies. (g) Therapists' experience and identification with the therapy they are required to deliver should be measured and matched across therapy groups.

SUMMARY

Family therapy is a general label that describes a variety of therapeutic approaches loosely grouped around the idea that the therapeutic target is change to the family system or one of its subsystems. Strangely, reviews usually include marital therapy but exclude most research on the behavioral family interventions for childhood disorders, leading to skewed conclusions about the state of the field. Research has supported the effectiveness of family therapy in general, with the most support found for behavioral-systems interventions for child conduct problems and parent-adolescent conflict. However, the quality of research has been highly variable and, in many cases, a clinical folklore has developed in the absence of any empirical support.

9

CONCLUSIONS AND
FUTURE DIRECTIONS

LEARNING FROM THE PAST

We have traveled a relatively short yet complex path both in this book and in the history of family research and therapy itself. It is clear that a wealth of research and clinical experience points to the importance of the family in the development of childhood behavioral and emotional problems. However, it is also clear that the quality and quantity of this evidence vary greatly according to the types of childhood disturbance and family characteristics under consideration. Family interaction patterns characterized by aggression, anxiety, and depression appear to facilitate the development of these characteristics in children; that is, children learn a behavioral repertoire and cognitive style that is a representation or internalization of the broader family style. However, research has not supported specific links between more general characteristics of family systems and child disturbances. In some cases, this is because the ideas about family systems are largely clinical folklore. In other cases, contemporary ideas about family systems may be accurate but our research methods either haven't been applied or are not sophisticated enough to evaluate such complex ideas.

The aim of this final chapter is to draw some general conclusions about the state of the field and to suggest directions for the path family researchers and clinicians take as we move into the next century. Throughout this summary, we will reflect on some of the most creative and innovative directions in the child and family area, research that appears to offer the best examples of what has been achieved to date and that provides optimism about and direction to what can be achieved in the near future. As we will see, most of the directions for future research that will be discussed involve the integration of the family approach with that of individual vulnerabilities for dysfunction and psychopathology. Furthermore, it will be seen that many of these new directions have come from research outside of the family area.

INTEGRATING SYSTEMIC AND INDIVIDUAL APPROACHES

Most schools of family theory and therapy have made explicit their disdain for the use of intrapsychic or biological models of dysfunction that focus attention on the individual out of his or her social context (see Becvar & Becvar, 1993). However, the family area risks becoming outdated and disconnected from the other sciences if this continues. Some reasons for this are as follows.

1. There is sufficient evidence to support a significant genetic factor in the transmission of vulnerabilities for particular psychological disorders (Rutter et al., 1990). Individuals differ in the degree they are characterized by cognitive, emotional, behavioral, and physiological processes that are markers for the specific vulnerability.

2. Much of the evidence for the involvement of family factors in the development of psychopathology shows that the important family factors are limited to, and functionally linked to, the specific types of behavioral problems found in the different forms or dimensions of the disorder. Thus families of depressed children show markers of depression throughout the family system but little evidence of other systemic disturbance.

3. There is little evidence to show that disturbances in family systems can actually drive development of psychopathology. Rather, the family system either becomes entangled in the problem, thus serving to perpetuate or alleviate the problem, or is simply a product of having a family member who is disturbed.

When family therapists talk about concepts such as enmeshment, family imbalance, chaotic family systems, and the like, they are referring to general family dynamics that are thought to be general risk factors for disturbance in individual family members. Data showing that these concepts are differentially related to different forms of disturbance have not been forthcoming and this has led family systems researchers to invoke concepts such as multifinality to account for them. This idea holds that the same stressor can lead to different outcomes. Of course, on its own, this idea does not contribute much in terms of direction for research. But, given that multifinality of outcomes may be due to variations in individual vulnerabilities, a more productive outcome may be had.

Consider the example of marital discord in parents. This has been shown to be a risk factor for a range of behavioral disturbances in children (Emery, 1982). Children are not generally happy living in households marked by marital conflict and separation. But why might some children develop anxiety problems, some aggression, and some children appear not to be affected at all? Clearly, each child's pattern of vulnerabilities will influence the outcome, and these vulnerabilities will be determined in part by the child's genetic heritage, his or her current physical and mental coping skills, his or her access to other social support, and his or her information and emotion processing style.

CREATIVE USES OF BEHAVIORAL OBSERVATIONS

There is enormous unrealized potential in the use of direct observations of children interacting with their families. Enormous progress has been made in this regard with respect to externalizing problems in children (e.g., Patterson, 1982); however, little of this type of research has been conducted with internalizing problems such as anxiety and depression in children. Further, expanding the role of these observations beyond their current role as dependent measures used to validate self-report measures and evaluate treatment success is a major priority. Two major areas for development suggest themselves. Let us take the example of anxiety.

First, there is the need to understand the child's anxiety in terms of its social context. Thus observation systems that score both the child's anxiety as well as other contextual, antecedent, and consequent stimuli need to be developed. Second, observations need to be designed and used in a way that allows for conceptual integration with other aspects of anxiety such as cognitive processing style, family interaction, and physiological reactivity. Third, when conducting observations of family interaction, researchers should code behavior in real time sequences, allowing for interdependencies between two or more people's behavior to be examined, as well as using more global ratings of behavior. Fourth, more energy should be directed to more complex and generalized forms of behavior disturbance than unilateral problems such as noncompliance and simple phobic states.

ADOPTING A BROADER
VIEW OF CHILD PSYCHOPATHOLOGY

The concept of psychopathology is fraught with conceptual and methodological problems, and never more so than when it is considered in a developmental framework with reference to children. The twentieth century has witnessed a constant struggle for the supremacy of medical/biological versus psychosocial models of psychopathology. As we approach the next century, an integrative approach is emerging; however, the growing dominance of a categorical/medical approach to psychopathology is evident despite a lack of evidence for the reliability and validity of this approach with children, and despite growing evidence that child behavioral and emotional problems are inseparable from the social context in which they occur.

The heated debates about the sociology of psychiatry and the dangers of labeling theory that occurred in the 1960s have largely disappeared from the literature, and there is a danger that categorical systems such as the *DSM-III-R* are generating their own validity through common usage rather than a firm scientific basis. Additional critical and creative research is needed into the validity of our basic assumptions about psychopathology with particular reference to normal developmental patterns and sequences, diagnostics, and the social context in which they occur.

ADOPTING A BROADER
VIEW OF CAUSALITY

Most family theorists see the rise of systems and family models of psychopathology as a subset of a major paradigm shift that is occurring in the social and physical sciences. The essence of this (arguable) revolutionary shift is an expanded view of causality. Theorists in support of this revolution see a progressive move from the bottom-up, linear causality of the logico-positivist approach of physical sciences since Newton to a circular, interactive causality embraced by modern information and systems sciences.

Traditionally, the physical sciences have progressed on the assumption that natural phenomena can be explained by a reductionistic, bottom-up approach. Analysis is aimed at the most basic processes detectable, and causality is seen to move upward from these processes. Thus it was assumed that natural phenomena could be best understood by studying basic atomic and molecular processes. In the social sciences, the first half of the century was dominated by a general behaviorism in which it was assumed that, like the physical sciences, behavior could best be understood by studying its basic processes, such as learning and individual biology. Again, causality was "bottom up" in that complex behavior and social organization could best be understood by understanding basic learning processes (e.g., Skinner, 1953).

Various streams of thought have challenged this focus on basic processes as the driving force in natural phenomena, and the family systems theorists have made a substantial contribution to this movement. The basic idea is that any system has basic properties and processes that drive (exert causal influence) the system upward, and "emergent" properties that, in turn, drive the system downward. Sperry (1993) has recently summarized this approach to the science of intelligence. The traditional neurosciences have approached the problem of intelligence using a bottom-up positivist assumption that brain activity, intelligence, thought, and so on are all reducible to the basic neurochemical processes of the brain. Sperry argues that the new information revolution accepts this bottom-up causal drive but also recognizes that the nervous system is a system that has emergent properties (consciousness) that also drive the system downward.

Similarly, a commonality of the family systems models has been their insistence that causality works both ways, reciprocally, in the relationship between the family and its members. Thus the family is a product of its constituent members, but the family will also be characterized by emergent properties such as rule systems, and rules that guide rule systems, and hierarchies that exert downward causal influence on the constituent parts.

This is the sort of creative thinking that is essential to the progress of humanity and, as Sperry (1993) has argued, these new ideas are appearing in all branches of science. But the family therapy movement has had little impact on, and even little cross-fertilization with, the other sciences. Perhaps the reason for this is that there has been a tendency for family theorists to "throw the baby out with the bath water." Along with the rejection of the (probably overstereotyped) unidirectional causality of the logico-positivist sciences, the family therapy movement has tended to reject the basic tools of science lock, stock, and barrel. Thus the family therapy field has been full of theorizing and the invention of new terms but very light on the development of new methods.

A major priority is thus the recognition that the new ideas that family systems and information models of human behavior have developed and embraced are at the forefront of science and are rapidly being incorporated into a new scientific view. Cross-fertilization with the other sciences will only help progress, and the more family models rest on untested and untestable theories, the quicker they will become redundant and outdated. The traditional scientific methods of hypothesis, observation, and replication are tools that can be used to great advantage without having to fully embrace the philosophy of science that was associated with their development.

LESSENING THE UNBALANCED FOCUS ON MOTHERS

On the whole, mothers have not been treated fairly by the mental health sciences of the twentieth century. To the contrary, fathers have generally escaped the focus of the behavioral sciences interested in parent-child relationships and their effects on children's adjustment. This focus on mothers has resulted from commission—that is, theories that hold, a priori, that the mother-child relationship is primary—to omission, where mothers have been the representatives of "parents" simply because they are easier to access for research and clinical purposes.

Research has increasingly demonstrated the importance of the father in traditional family structures (e.g., Lamb, 1981) and increasing effort needs to be given to assigning equitable attention to both parents in future research in child development and family process.

IMPROVING THE QUALITY OF RESEARCH

In Chapters 6 and 7, the common research designs were reviewed as well as recommendations for maximizing the quality of these designs. The field of family therapy, with the exception of the more behavioral streams, has not devoted much energy to empirical verification of its theories and methods. Rather, it has been content to derive its status from the fame and prestige of some of its leading practitioners and writers. The fault for this lies in both camps. Family therapists have taken an easy path in accepting truisms and clinical folklore as the basis of the area. But they have also been partly justified in rejecting the modern scientific tradition as not being appropriate to their model. That is, operationalizing concepts into a form in which they can be measured with numbers often destroys the subtlety and complexity of those concepts. At present, many of the methods of the behavioral sciences are simply not precise and subtle enough to capture the intricacies of human behavior.

However, this does not mean that the scientific method should be abandoned or that family therapy is irrelevant and too "soft" to contribute to the general evolution of science. On the contrary, some of the major contemporary issues of modern science can be seen in a particularly salient form in the child and family area. These include the idea of complex and reciprocal causality, systemic interdependency, and the evolution of patterns in complex systems. Cross-fertilization between the family area and a clinical research perspective has the potential to make a major contribution to these exciting issues.

FAMILIES AS PROTECTIVE SYSTEMS: A FAMILY EMPOWERMENT MODEL

Much of the emphasis in this book has been on clinical aspects of child development and the family—that is, when things go wrong. As we have seen, this emphasis on the family as a "cause" of childhood problems has permeated the history of the family therapy movement. In the middle of the twentieth century, extreme views were presented and used in therapies. Families, and usually mothers within the family, were seen as a negative influence on children, and the job of the therapist was to change the family, or help the child individuate from the family, so the "victim" child could reach his or her full, unhampered potential.

These extremes have increasingly been replaced by a more compassionate model in which families are seen as the natural support systems for developing children—assets of the community—and as allies of the mental health professionals who share a commitment to the well-being of children. For example, models of the family causes of schizophrenia that dominated the 1960s have largely been replaced by psychoeducational models that seek to empower the family in the difficult job of caring for a mentally ill person in the community.

The empowerment of families should be a major goal of all family therapies. Through the active sharing of knowledge and power with families at the administrative, clinical, and interpersonal levels, family therapists and researchers can help create a united front working for the increasing welfare and potentialities of children.

REFERENCES

Achenbach, T. M., & Edelbrock, C. S. (1991). *Manual for the Child Behavior Checklist and the Revised Child Behavior Profile.* Burlington, VT: University Associates in Psychiatry.

Ackerman, N. (1938). The unity of the family. *Archives of Pediatrics, 55,* 51-62.

Ainsworth, M. D. S. (1989). Attachment beyond infancy. *American Psychologist, 44,* 709-716.

Ainsworth, M. D. S., Blehar, M. C., Waters, E., & Wall, S. (1978). *Patterns of attachment: A psychological study of the strange situation.* Hillsdale, NJ: Erlbaum.

Alexander, J. F., & Parsons, B. V. (1973). Short term behavioral intervention with delinquent families: Impact on family process and recidivism. *Journal of Abnormal Psychology, 81,* 219-225.

American Psychiatric Association. (1987). *Diagnostic and statistical manual of mental disorders* (3rd ed., rev.). Washington, DC: Author.

Anderson, J., Williams, S., McGee, R., & Silva, P. A. (1987). The prevalence of DSM-III disorders in a large sample of preadolescent children from the general population. *Archives of General Psychiatry, 44,* 69-76.

Apley, J. (1975). *The child with abdominal pains* (2nd ed.). Oxford: Blackwell.

Atoynatan, T. H. (1986). Elective mutism: Involvement of the mother in the treatment of the child. *Child Psychiatry and Human Development, 17,* 15-27.

Badia, P., Huber, A., & Runyon, R. (1970). *Research problems in psychology.* Reading, MA: Addison-Wesley.

Barkley, R. A., Guevremont, D. C., Anastopoulos, A. D., & Fletcher, K. E. (1992). A comparison of three family therapy programs for treating family conflict in adolescents with ADHD. *Journal of Consulting and Clinical Psychology, 60,* 450-462.

Barrett, P. M., Dadds, M. R., Rapee, R. M., & Ryan, S. (1993, November). *Cognitive-behavioral and family therapy for childhood anxiety disorders: A controlled trial.* Paper presented at the annual convention of the Association for the Advancement of Behavior Therapy, Atlanta.

Barrett, P. M., Rapee, R. M., Dadds, M. R., & Ryan, S. (1993, November). *Threat perception and family context in the development of childhood anxiety.* Paper presented at the annual convention of the Association for the Advancement of Behavior Therapy, Atlanta.

Bateson, G., Jackson, D. D., Haley, J., & Weakland, J. (1956). Towards a theory of schizophrenia. *Behavioral Science, 1,* 251-264.

Beach, S. R. H., Sandeen, E. E., & O'Leary, K. D. (1990). *Depression in marriage.* New York: Guilford.

Beautrais, A. L., Fergusson, D. M., & Shannon, F. T. (1982). Family life events and behavioral problems in preschool children. *Pediatrics, 70,* 774-779.

Beck, A. T., Ward, C. H., Mendelson, M., Mock, J., & Erbaugh, J. (1961). An inventory for measuring depression. *Archives of General Psychiatry, 4,* 561-571.

Becvar, D. S., & Becvar, R. J. (1993). *Family therapy: A systemic integration* (2nd ed.). New York: Allyn & Bacon.

Bednar, R. L., Burlingame, G. M., & Masters, K. S. (1988). Systems of family treatment: Substance or semantics. *Annual Review of Psychology, 39,* 401-434.

Bernstein, G. A., & Borchardt, C. M. (1991). Anxiety disorders of childhood and adolescence: A critical review. *Journal of the American Academy of Child and Adolescent Psychiatry, 30,* 519-532.

Billings, A. G., & Moos, R. H. (1983). Comparisons of children of depressed and non-depressed parents: A social environmental perspective. *Journal of Abnormal Child Psychology, 11,* 463-486.

Birchwood, M., & Smith, J. (1987). Schizophrenia and the family. In J. Orford (Ed.), *Coping with disorder in the family* (pp. 7-38). London: Croom Helm.

Blechman, E. A. (1982). Are children with one parent at psychological risk: A methodological review. *Journal of Marriage and the Family, 44,* 179-195.

Blechman, E. A. (1984). Competent parents, competent children: Behavioral objectives of parent training. In R. F. Dangel & R. A. Polster (Eds.), *Parent training: Foundations of research and practice* (pp. 34-63). New York: Guilford.

Blechman, E. A., & McEnroe, M. J. (1985). Effective family problem solving. *Child Development, 56,* 429-437.

Bowlby, D. (1973). *Attachment and loss II: Separation.* New York: Basic Books.

Bowlby, D. (1980). *Attachment and loss I: Attachment.* New York: Basic Books. (Original work published 1969)

Bowlby, D. (1982). *Attachment and loss III: Loss.* New York: Basic Books.

Brady, E. U., & Kendall, P. C. (1992). Comorbidity of anxiety and depression in children and adolescents. *Psychological Bulletin, 111,* 244-255.

Brewin, C. R. (1987). *Cognitive foundations of clinical psychology.* London: Erlbaum.

Brewin, C. R., MacCarthy, B., Duda, K., & Vaughn, C. E. (1991). Attribution and expressed emotion in the relatives of patients with schizophrenia. *Journal of Abnormal Psychology, 100,* 546-554.

Brody, G. H., & Forehand, R. (1985). The efficacy of parent training with maritally distressed and nondistressed mothers: A multimethod assessment. *Behavioral Research and Therapy, 23,* 291-296.

Bronfenbrenner, U. (1977). Towards an experimental ecology of human development. *American Psychologist, 32,* 513-531.

Brown, G. W., Birley, J. L. T., & Wing, J. K. (1972). The influence of family life on schizophrenic disorders: A replication. *British Journal of Psychiatry, 121,* 241-258.

Bruch, H. (1973). *Eating disorders: Obesity, anorexia nervosa and the person within.* New York: Basic Books.

Brunk, M., Henggeler, S. W., & Whelan, J. P. (1987). Comparison of multisystemic therapy and parent training in the brief treatment of child abuse and neglect. *Journal of Consulting and Clinical Psychology, 55,* 171-178.

Chambers, W. J., Puig-Antich, J., Hirsch, M., Paez, P., Ambrosini, P. J., Tabrizi, M. A., & Davies, M. (1985). The assessment of affective disorders in children and adolescents by semi-structured interview: Test-retest reliability. *Archives of General Psychiatry, 42,* 696-702.

Christoff, K. A., & Myatt, R. J. (1987). Social isolation. In M. Hersen & V. B. Van Hasselt (Eds.), *Behavior therapy with children and adolescents: A clinical approach* (pp. 512-536). New York: John Wiley.

Cole, C., & Morrow, W. R. (1981). Refractory parent behaviors in behavior modification training groups. *Psychotherapy: Theory, Research and Practice, 13,* 162-169.

Cole, D. A., & Rehm, L. P. (1986). Family interaction patterns and childhood depression. *Journal of Abnormal Child Psychology, 14,* 297-314.

Connell, H. M. (1972). Depression in childhood. *Child Psychiatry and Human Development, 4,* 71-85.

Coyne, J. C. (1976). Toward an interactional description of depression. *Psychiatry, 39,* 28-40.

Crisp, A. H. (1980). *Anorexia nervosa: Let me be.* London: Academic Press.

Crisp, A. H., Harding, B., & McGuiness, B. (1974). Anorexia nervosa: Psychoneurotic characteristics: Relationship to prognosis. A quantitative study. *Journal of Psychosomatic Research, 18,* 167-173.

Crook, T., Riskin, A., & Eliot, J. (1981). Parent-child relationship and adult depression. *Child Development, 52,* 950-957.

Cytryn, L., & McKnew, D. H. (1974). Factors influencing the changing clinical expression of the depressive process in children. *American Journal of Psychiatry, 131,* 879-881.

• Dadds, M. (1987). Families and the origins of child behavior problems. *Family Process, 26,* 341-357.

Dadds, M. R. (1989). Child behavior therapy and family context. *Child and Family Behavior Therapy, 11,* 27-44.

Dadds, M. R., Adlington, F., & Christensen, A. (1987). Children's perceptions of time out and other parental disciplinary strategies. *Behaviour Change, 4,* 3-13.

Dadds, M. R., Barrett, P. M., Rapee, R. M., & Ryan, S. (1993, November). *Family processes in childhood anxiety.* Paper presented at the annual convention of the Association for the Advancement of Behavior Therapy, Atlanta.

Dadds, M. R., & McHugh, T. (1992). Social support and treatment outcome in behavioral family therapy for child conduct problems. *Journal of Consulting and Clinical Psychology, 60,* 252-259.

Dadds, M. R., & Powell, M. B. (1991). The relationship of interparental conflict and marital adjustment to aggression, anxiety and immaturity in aggressive and nonclinic children. *Journal of Abnormal Child Psychology, 19,* 553-567.

Dadds, M. R., Rapee, R. M., & Barrett, P. M. (in press). Behavioral observation. In T. H. Ollendick, N. J. King, & W. Yule (Eds.), *International handbook of phobic and anxiety disorders of children.* New York: Plenum.

Dadds, M. R., Rapee, R. M., & Heard, P. M. (1991). Anxiety disorders in children. *International Review of Psychiatry, 3,* 231-241.

Dadds, M. R., Sanders, M. R., Behrens, B. C., & James, J. E. (1987). Marital discord and child behaviour problems: A description of family interactions during treatment. *Journal of Clinical Child Psychology, 16,* 192-203.

Dadds, M. R., Sanders, M. R., Morrison, M., & Rebgetz, M. (1992). Child depression and conduct disorder II: An analysis of family interactions in the home. *Journal of Abnormal Psychology, 101,* 505-513.

Dadds, M. R., Schwartz, S., & Sanders, M. R. (1987). Marital discord and treatment outcome in the treatment of childhood conduct disorders. *Journal of Consulting and Clinical Psychology, 55,* 396-403.

Dadds, M. R., Sheffield, J. K., & Holbeck, J. F. (1990). An examination of the differential relationship of marital discord to parents' discipline strategies for boys and girls. *Journal of Abnormal Child Psychology, 18,* 121-129.

Doane, J. (1985). Parental communication deviance and offspring psychopathology. In L. L'Abate (Ed.), *The handbook of family psychology and therapy* (Vol. 2, pp. 937-959). Homewood, IL: Dorsey.

Dodge, K. A. (1985). Attributional bias in aggressive children. In P. C. Kendall (Ed.), *Advances in cognitive-behavioral research and therapy* (Vol. 4, pp. 73-110). Orlando, FL: Academic Press.

Donovan, W. L., Leavitt, L. A., & Balling, J. D. (1978). Maternal psychological response to infant signals. *Psychophysiology, 15,* 68-74.

Downey, G., & Coyne, J. C. (1990). Children of depressed parents: An integrative review. *Psychological Bulletin, 108,* 50-76.

Dumas, J. E. (1989). Interact: A computer based coding and data management system to assess family interactions. In R. J. Prinz (Ed.), *Advances in the behavioral assessment of children and families* (Vol. 3, pp. 177-202). Greenwich, CT: JAI.

Dumas, J. E., & Wahler, R. G. (1983). Predictors of treatment outcome in parent training: Mother insularity and socioeconomic disadvantage. *Behavioral Assessment, 5,* 301-313.

Elder, G. H., Nguyen, T. V., & Caspi, A. (1985). Linking family hardship to children's lives. *Developmental Psychology, 56,* 361-375.

• Emery, R. E. (1982). Interparental conflict and the children of discord and divorce. *Psychological Bulletin, 9,* 310-330.

Emery, R. E., & O'Leary, K. D. (1982). Children's perceptions of marital discord and behaviour problems of boys and girls. *Journal of Abnormal Child Psychology, 10,* 11-24.

Emery, R. E., Weintraub, S., & Neale, J. M. (1982). Effects of marital discord on the school behavior of children of schizophrenic, affectively disordered and normal parents. *Journal of Abnormal Child Psychology, 10,* 215-218.

Falloon, I. R. H., Boyd, J. L., McGill, C. W., Williamson, M., et al. (1985). Family management in the prevention of morbidity of schizophrenia: Clinical outcome of a two year longitudinal study. *Archives of General Psychiatry, 42,* 887-896.

Fergusson, D. M., Horwood, L. J., & Shannon, F. T. (1984). A proportional hazards model of family breakdown. *Journal of Marriage and the Family, 46,* 539-549.

Forehand, R. L., & Atkeson, B. M. (1977). Generality of treatment effects with parents as therapists. *Behavior Therapy, 8,* 575-593.

Forehand, R., Brody, G., Slotkin, J., Fauber, R., McCombs, A., & Long, N. (1988). Young adolescent and maternal depression: Assessment, interrelations, and predictors. *Journal of Consulting and Clinical Psychology, 56,* 422-426.

Forehand, R. L., & Long, N. (1988). Outpatient treatment of the acting out child: Procedures, long term follow-up data, and clinical problems. *Advances in Behavior Research and Therapy, 10,* 129-177.

Framo, D. L. (1975). Personal reflections of a therapist. *Journal of Marriage and Family Counseling, 1,* 15-28.

Fromm-Reichmann, F. (1948). Notes on the development of schizophrenics by psychoanalytic psychiatry. *Psychiatry, 11,* 263-273.

Furey, W. M., & Basili, L. A. (1988). Predicting consumer satisfaction in parent training for noncompliant children. *Behavior Therapy, 19,* 555-564.

Garfinkel, P. E., & Garner, D. M. (1982). *Anorexia nervosa: A multidimensional perspective.* New York: Brunner/Mazel.

Garralda, M. E., & Bailey, D. (1986). Children with psychiatric disorders in primary care. *Journal of Child Psychology & Psychiatry, 27,* 611-624.

Gehring, T. M., & Marti, D. (1993). The Family Systems Test: Differences in perception of family structures between nonclinical and clinical children. *Journal of Child Psychology and Psychiatry, 34,* 363-377.

Goldenberg, I., & Goldenberg, H. (1985). *Family therapy: An overview* (2nd ed.). Monterey, CA: Brooks/Cole.

Goldstein, A. P., Keller, H., & Erne, D. (1985). *Changing the abusive parent.* Champaign, IL: Research Press.

Goldstein, M. J. (1981). Family factors associated with schizophrenia and anorexia nervosa. *Journal of Youth and Adolescence, 10,* 385-405.

Goodyer, I. N. (1990). Family relationships, life events and child psychopathology. *Journal of Child Psychology and Psychiatry, 31,* 161-192.

Green, S. M., Loeber, R., & Lahey, B. B. (1992). Child psychopathology and deviant family hierarchies. *Journal of Child and Family Studies, 1,* 341-350.

Griest, D. L., Forehand, R., Rogers, T., Breiner, J., Furey, W., & Williams, C. A. (1982). Effects of parent enhancement therapy on the treatment outcome and generalisation of a parent training program. *Behavior Research and Therapy, 20,* 429-436.

Griest, D. L., & Wells, K. C. (1983). Behavioral family therapy with conduct disorders in children. *Behavior Therapy, 20,* 429-436.

Grych, J. H., & Fincham, F. D. (1990). Marital conflict and children's adjustment: A cognitive-contextual framework. *Psychological Bulletin, 108,* 267-290.

Guerin, P. J. (1976). Family therapy: The first twenty five years. In P. J. Guerin (Ed.), *Family therapy: Theory and practice* (pp. 1-33). New York: Gardner.

Gurman, A. S. (1979). Dimensions of marital therapy: A comparative analysis. *Journal of Marital and Family Therapy, 5,* 5-18.

Gurman, A. S., Kniskern, D. P., & Pinsof, W. M. (1986). Research on the process and outcome of marital and family therapy. In S. Garfield & A. Bergin (Eds.), *Handbook of psychotherapy and behavior change* (3rd ed.). New York: Wiley.

Haley, J. (1976). *Problem solving therapy.* New York: Harper Colophon.

Haley, J., & Hoffman, L. (1967). *Techniques of family therapy.* New York: Basic Books.

Hare-Mustin, R. T. (1978). A feminist approach to family therapy. *Family Process, 17,* 181-194.

Harrison, C., Dadds, M. R., Smith, G., & Baglioni, A. J. (1994). *An attributional model of critical response in caregivers of schizophrenic patients.* Paper under review.

Hayes, H. (1991). A reintroduction to family therapy: Clarification of three schools. *Australian and New Zealand Journal of Family Therapy, 12,* 27-43.

Hazelrigg, M. D., Cooper, H. M., & Borduin, C. M. (1987). Evaluating the effectiveness of family therapies: An integrative review and analysis. *Psychological Review, 101,* 428-442.

Heard, P. M., Dadds, M. R., & Conrad, P. (1992). Assessment and treatment of simple phobias in children: A clinical study. *Behaviour Change, 9,* 73-82.

Hersen, M., & Barlow, D. H. (1976). *Single case experimental designs.* New York: Pergamon.

Hetherington, E. M., Cox, M., & Cox, A. (1982). Effects of divorce on parents and children. In M. E. Lamb (Ed.), *Nontraditional families* (pp. 223-288). Hillsdale, NJ: Erlbaum.

Hetherington, E. M., & Martin, B. (1979). Family interaction. In H. C. Quay & J. S. Werry (Eds.), *Psychopathological disorders of childhood* (pp. 30-82). New York: Wiley.

Hoffman, L. (1981). *The foundations of family therapy.* New York: Basic Books.

Holtzman, W. H. (1976). Inkblots through the looking glass. In M. H. Siegel & H. P. Zeigler (Eds.), *Psychological research: The inside story* (pp. 306-321). New York: Harper & Row.

Hooley, J. M. (1987). The nature and origins of expressed emotion. In K. Hahlweg & M. J. Goldstein (Eds.), *Understanding major mental disorder: The contribution of family interaction research.* New York: Family Process Press.

Hops, H., Biglan, A., Sherman, L., Arthur, J., Friedman, L., & Osteen, V. (1987). Home observations of family interactions of depressed women. *Journal of Consulting and Clinical Psychology, 55,* 341-346.

Humphrey, L. L. (1989). Observed family interactions among subtypes of eating disorder using structural analysis social behavior. *Journal of Consulting and Clinical Psychology, 57,* 206-214.

Jacobsen, N. S., & Margolin, G. (1979). *Marital therapy: Strategies based on social learning and behavior exchange principles.* New York: Brunner/Mazel.

Julien, D., Markman, H. J., & Lindahl, K. M. (1989). A comparison of a global and a microanalytic coding system: Implications for future trends in studying interactions. *Behavioral Assessment, 11,* 81-100.

Kagan, J., Reznick, J. S., & Snidman, N. (1988). Biological bases of childhood shyness. *Science, 240,* 167-171.

Kantor, D., & Lehr, W. (1975). *Inside the family.* San Francisco: Jossey-Bass.

Kashani, J. H., Orvaschel, H., Rosenberg, T. K., & Reid, J. C. (1989). Psychopathology in a community sample of children and adolescents: A developmental perspective. *Journal of the American Academy of Child and Adolescent Psychiatry, 28,* 701-706.

Kaslow, F. W. (1987). Marital and family therapy. In M. B. Sussman & S. K. Steinmetz (Eds.), *Handbook of marriage and the family* (pp. 81-102). New York: Plenum.

Kazdin, A. E. (1987). *Conduct disorder in childhood and adolescents.* Newbury Park, CA: Sage.

Kazdin, A. E. (1988). The diagnosis of childhood disorders: Assessment issues and strategies. *Behavioral Assessment, 10,* 67-94.

Kazdin, A. E. (1990). Childhood depression. *Journal of Child Psychology and Psychiatry, 31,* 121-160.

Keith, D. V., & Whitaker, C. A. (1982). Experiential/symbolic family therapy. In A. M. Horne & M. M. Ohlsen (Eds.), *Family counseling and therapy.* Itasca, IL: F. E. Peacock.

Kendall, P. C. (Ed.). (1991). [Special issue on clinical significance]. *Journal of Consulting and Clinical Psychology, 59.*

Koegel, R. L., Glahn, T. J., & Nieminen, G. S. (1978). Generalization of parent training results. *Journal of Applied Behavior Analysis, 11,* 95-109.

Lahey, B. B., Hartdagen, S. E., Frick, P. J., McBurnett, K., Connor, R., & Hynd, G. W. (1988). Conduct disorder: Parsing the confounded relationship to a parental divorce and antisocial personality. *Journal of Abnormal Psychology, 97,* 334-337.

Laing, R. D., & Esterson, A. (1974). *Sanity, madness and the family.* London: Tavistock. (Original work published 1964)

Lamb, M. (1981). *The role of the father in child development.* New York: Wiley.

Lamb, M., & Elster, A. B. (1985). Adolescent mother-infant-father relationships. *Developmental Psychology, 21,* 768-773.

Lazarus, R. S., & Folkman, S. (1984). *Stress, appraisal and coping.* New York: Springer.

Lefkowitz, M. M., & Tesiny, E. P. (1985). Depression in children: Prevalence and correlates. *Journal of Consulting and Clinical Psychology, 53,* 647-656.

Le Grange, D., Eisler, I., Dare, C., & Hodes, M. (1992). Family criticism and self-starvation: A study of expressed emotion. *Journal of Family Therapy, 14,* 177-192.

Liberman, R. (1970). Behavioral approaches to family and couple therapy. *American Journal of Orthopsychiatry, 40,* 106-118.

Lochman, J. E. (1990). Modification of childhood aggression. In M. Hersen, R. M. Eisler, & P. Miller (Eds.), *Progress in behavior modification* (Vol. 2, pp. 47-85). New York: Academic Press.

Loeber, R. (1990). Development and risk factors of juvenile antisocial behavior and delinquency. *Clinical Psychology Review, 10,* 1-41.

Lutzker, J. (1984). Project 12 Ways: Treating child abuse and neglect from an ecobehavioral perspective. In R. F. Dangel & R. A. Polster (Eds.), *Parent training: Foundations of research and practice* (pp. 260-291). New York: Guilford.

Madanes, C., Duke, J., & Harbin, H. (1980). Family ties of heroin addicts. *Archives of General Psychiatry, 37,* 889-902.

Madden, D. J., & Harbin, H. T. (1983). Family structures of assaultive adolescents. *Journal of Marital and Family Therapy, 9,* 311-316.

McGuire, J., & Richman, N. (1986). The prevalence of behavioral problems in three types of preschool group. *Journal of Child Psychology & Psychiatry, 27,* 455-472.

McMahon, R. J., & Forehand, R. (1983). Consumer satisfaction in behavioral treatment of children: Types, issues, and recommendations. *Behavior Therapy, 14,* 209-225.

Miklowitz, D. J., Goldstein, M. J., Falloon, I. R. H., & Doane, J. A. (1984). Interactional correlates of expressed emotion in the families of schizophrenics. *British Journal of Psychiatry, 144,* 482-487.

Miller, G. E., & Prinz, R. J. (1990). Enhancement of social learning family interventions for childhood conduct disorder. *Psychological Bulletin, 108,* 291-307.

Minuchin, S. (1974). *Families and family therapy.* Cambridge, MA: Harvard University Press.

Minuchin, S., & Fishman, H. C. (1981). *Family therapy techniques.* Cambridge, MA: Harvard University Press.

Minuchin, S., Montalvo, B., Guerney, B., Rosman, B., & Schumer, F. (1967). *Families of the slums.* New York: Basic Books.

Minuchin, S., Rosman, B. L., & Baker, L. (1978). *Psychosomatic families: Anorexia nervosa in context.* Cambridge, MA: Harvard University Press.

Moos, R. H. (1974). *The Family, Work & Group Environment Scales manual.* Palo Alto, CA: Consulting Psychologists Press.

Mullins, L. L., Siegel, L. J., & Hodges, K. (1985). Cognitive problem solving and life event correlates of depressive symptoms in children. *Journal of Abnormal Child Psychology, 13,* 305-314.

O'Connor, W. A., & Stachowiak, J. (1971). Patterns of interaction in families with high adjusted, low adjusted and mentally retarded members. *Family Process, 10,* 229-241.

Ollendick, T. H., & Hersen, M. (1984). *Child behavioral assessment: Principles and procedures.* New York: Pergamon.

Olson, D. H., Portner, J., & Bell, R. (1982). *Faces II: Family Adaptability and Cohesion Evaluation Scales.* St. Paul: University of Minnesota, Family Social Science.

Olson, D. H., Russell, C., & Sprenkle, D. H. (1983). Circumplex model of marital and family systems: VI. Theoretical update. *Family Process, 22,* 69-83.

Orford, J. (1987). *Coping with disorder in the family.* London: Croom Helm.

Palmer, R. L., Marshall, P., & Oppenheimer, R. (1987). Anorexia and the family. In J. Orford (Ed.), *Coping with disorder in the family* (pp. 117-137). London: Croom Helm.

Parker, G. (1989). The Parental Bonding Instrument: Psychometric properties reviewed. *Psychiatric Developments, 4,* 317-335.

Parker, J. G., & Asher, S. R. (1987). Peer relations and later personal adjustment: Are low-accepted children at risk? *Psychological Bulletin, 102,* 357-389.

Parsons, B. V., & Alexander, J. F. (1973). Short term family intervention: A therapy outcome study. *Journal of Consulting and Clinical Psychology, 41,* 195-201.

Parsons, T. (1951). *The social system.* Glencoe, IL: Free Press.

Patterson, G. R. (1982). *Coercive family process.* Eugene, OR: Castalia.

Patterson, G. R. (1986). Performance models for antisocial boys. *American Psychologist, 41,* 432-444.

Patterson, G. R., & Reid, J. B. (1984). Social interactional processes in the family: The study of the moment by moment family transactions in which human social development is embedded. *Journal of Applied Developmental Psychology, 5,* 237-262.

Paul, G. (1986). Can pregnancy be a placebo effect? *Journal of Behavior Therapy and Experimental Psychiatry, 17,* 61-81.

Piercy, F. P., & Sprenkle, D. H. (1990). Marriage and family therapy: A decade review. *Journal of Marriage and the Family, 52,* 1116-1126.

Porter, B., & O'Leary, K. D. (1980). Marital discord and childhood behaviour problems. *Journal of Abnormal Child Psychology, 80,* 287-295.

Procidano, M. E., & Heller, K. (1983). Measures of perceived social support from family and friends: Three validation studies. *American Journal of Community Psychology, 11,* 1-25.

Puig-Antich, J., Kaufman, J., Ryan, N. D., Williamson, D. E., Dahl, R. E., Lukens, E., Todak, G., Ambrosini, P., Rabinovich, H., & Nelson, B. (1993). The psychosocial functioning and family environment of depressed adolescents. *Journal of the American Academy of Child Psychiatry, 32,* 244-253.

Purcell, K., Brady, K., Chai, H., Muser, J., Molk, L., Gordon, N., & Means, J. (1969). The effects on asthma in children of experimental separation from the family. *Psychosomatic Medicine, 31,* 144-164.

Quay, H. C., & Peterson, D. R. (1983). *Manual for the Revised Behavior Problem Checklist.* Coral Gables, FL: University of Miami, Applied Social Sciences.

Rapee, R. M., Barrett, P. M., Dadds, M. R., & Evans, L. (in press). Reliability of the DSM-III-R childhood anxiety disorders using structured interview. *Journal of the American Academy of Child and Adolescent Psychiatry.*

Ratsam, M., & Gillberg, C. (1991). The family background in anorexia nervosa: A population based study. *Journal of the American Academy of Child Psychiatry, 30,* 283-289.

Robin, A. L. (1981). A controlled evaluation of problem solving communication training with parent-adolescent conflict. *Behavior Therapy, 12,* 593-609.

Robin, A. L., & Canter, W. (1984). A comparison of the marital interaction coding system and community ratings for assessing mother-adolescent problem solving. *Behavioral Assessment, 6,* 303-313.

Robin, A. L., & Foster, S. (1989). *Negotiating parent-adolescent conflict: A behavioral family systems approach.* New York: Guilford.

Rosenberg, J. B. (1978). Two is better than one: Use of behavioral techniques within a structured family therapy model. *Journal of Marriage and Family Counseling, 4,* 31-40.

Rosenhan, D. L., & Seligman, M. E. P. (1984). *Abnormal psychology.* New York: Norton.

Rutter, M. (1972). *Maternal deprivation reassessed.* Middlesex, U.K.: Penguin.

Rutter, M. (1989). Pathways from childhood to adult life. *Journal of Child Psychology and Psychiatry, 30,* 23-51.

110 THE DEVELOPMENT OF DYSFUNCTION

Rutter, M., Cox, A., Tupling, C., Berger, M., & Yule, W. (1975). Attainment in two geographical areas: 1. The prevalence of psychiatric disorder. *British Journal of Psychiatry, 126,* 493-509.

Rutter, M., McDonald, H., LeCouteur, A., Harrington, R., Bolton, P., & Bailey, A. (1990). Genetic factors in child psychiatric disorders: II. Empirical findings. *Journal of Child Psychology and Psychiatry, 31,* 39-83.

Sanders, M. R., & Christensen, A. (1985). A comparison of the effects of child management training and planned activities training in five parenting environments. *Journal of Abnormal Child Psychology, 13,* 101-117.

Sanders, M. R., & Dadds, M. R. (1982). The effects of planned activities and child management training: An analysis of setting generalization. *Behavioral Therapy, 13,* 1-11.

Sanders, M. R., & Dadds, M. R. (1993). *Behavioral family intervention.* New York: Longwood.

Sanders, M. R., Dadds, M. R., & Bor, W. (1989). A contextual analysis of oppositional child behavior and maternal aversive behavior in families of conduct disordered children. *Journal of Clinical Child Psychology, 18,* 72-83.

Sanders, M., Dadds, M., Johnston, R., & Cash, R. (1992). Child depression and conduct disorder: Cognitive constructions and family problem solving interactions. *Journal of Abnormal Psychology, 101,* 496-504.

Sanders, M. R., & Glynn, E. (1981). Training parents in behavioral self-management. *Journal of Applied Behavior Analysis, 14,* 223-237.

Sanders, M. R., & James, J. E. (1983). The modification of parent behavior: A review of generalization and maintenance. *Behavior Modification, 7,* 3-27.

Sanders, M. R., Patel, R., Le Gris, S., & Shepherd, R. (1990). *An observational analysis of family interactions during mealtimes in children with persistent feeding disorders.* Unpublished manuscript.

Sanders, M. R., Rebgetz, M., Morrison, M., Bor, W., Gordon, A., Dadds, M. R., & Shephard, R. (1989). Cognitive-behavioral treatment of recurrent nonspecific abdominal pain in children: An analysis of generalization and side effects. *Journal of Consulting and Clinical Psychology, 57,* 294-300.

Sanders, M. R., Rebgetz, M., Morrison, M., Bor, W., Gordon, A., Dadds, M. R., & Shephard, R. (1990). Behavioral treatment of childhood recurrent abdominal pain: Relationships between pain, children's characteristics and family functioning. *Behaviour Change, 7,* 16-24.

Schaffer, R. B. (1985). Effects of marital role problems on wife's depressed mood. *Journal of Consulting and Clinical Psychology, 53,* 541-554.

Scholom, A., Zucker, R. A., & Stollack, G. E. (1979). Relating early child adjustment to infant and parent temperament. *Journal of Abnormal Child Psychology, 7,* 297-308.

Schwartz, S. (1992). *Cases in abnormal psychology.* Brisbane, Australia: Wiley.

Selvini-Palazzoli, M. (1974). *Self starvation.* London: Chaucer.

Selvini-Palazzoli, M., Boscolo, L., Cecchin, G., & Prata, G. (1978). *Paradox and counter-paradox.* New York: Jason Aronson.

Silverman, W. K., & Nelles, W. B. (1988). The Anxiety Disorders Interview Schedule for Children. *Journal of the American Academy of Child and Adolescent Psychiatry, 27,* 772-778.

Sines, J. O. (1987). Influence of the home and family environment on childhood dysfunction. In B. B. Lahey & A. E. Kazdin (Eds.), *Advances in clinical child psychology* (Vol. 10, pp. 1-54). New York: Plenum.

Singer, M., & Wynne, L. (1965). Thought disorder and family relations of schizophrenics: IV. Results and implications. *Archives of General Psychiatry, 12*, 201-212.

Skinner, B. F. (1953). *Science and human behavior*. New York: Macmillan.

Spanier, G. B. (1976). Measuring dyadic adjustment. *Journal of Marriage and the Family, 38*, 15-28.

Sperry, R. W. (1993). The impact and promise of the cognitive revolution. *American Psychologist, 48*, 878-885.

Stark, K. D., Humphrey, L. L., Crook, K., & Lewis, K. (1990). Perceived family environments of depressed and anxious children. *Journal of Abnormal Child Psychology, 18*, 527-548.

Steiger, H., Liquornik, K., Chapman, J., & Hussain, N. (1991). Personality and family disturbances in eating-disorder patients. *International Journal of Eating Disorders, 10*, 501-512.

Straus, M. A. (1979). Measuring intrafamily conflict and violence: The Conflict Tactics Scale. *Journal of Marriage and the Family, 41*, 75-88.

Sussman, M. B., & Steinmetz, S. K. (Eds.). (1987). *Handbook of marriage and the family*. New York: Plenum.

Szykula, S. A., Morris, S. B., Sudweeks, C., & Saygar, T. V. (1987). Child focussed behavior and strategic therapy: Outcome comparison. *Psychotherapy, 35*, 546-551.

Terkelson, K. G. (1983). Schizophrenia and the family II: Adverse effects of family therapy. *Family Process, 22*, 191-200.

Thomas, D. L., & Wilcox, J. E. (1987). The rise of family theory: An historical and critical analysis. In M. B. Sussman & S. K. Steinmetz (Eds.), *Handbook of marriage and the family* (pp. 81-102). New York: Plenum.

Touliatos, J., Perlmutter, B., & Strauss, M. (Eds.). (1990). *Handbook of family measurement techniques*. Newbury Park, CA: Sage.

Tseng, W. W., & McDermott, J. F. (1979). Triaxial family classification. *Journal of the American Academy of Child Psychiatry, 18*, 22-43.

Vaughn, C. E., & Leff, J. P. (1976). The influence of family and social factors on the course of psychiatric illness: A comparison of schizophrenic and depressed neurotic patients. *British Journal of Psychiatry, 129*, 125-137.

Viken, A. (1985). Psychiatric epidemiology in a sample of 1510 ten year old children. 1: Prevalence. *Journal of Child Psychology & Psychiatry, 26*, 55-75.

Vygotsky, L. S. (1960). *Development of the higher mental functions*. Moscow: Nauk RSFSR.

Wahler, R. G. (1969). Oppositional children: A quest for parental reinforcement control. *Journal of Applied Behavior Analysis, 2*, 159-170.

Wahler, R. G. (1980). The insular mother: Her problems in parent-child treatment. *Journal of Applied Behavior Analysis, 13*, 207-219.

Wahler, R. G., & Afton, A. D. (1980). Attentional processes in insular and noninsular mothers. *Child Behavior Therapy, 2*, 25-41.

Wahler, R. G., & Graves, M. G. (1983). Setting events in social networks: Ally or enemy in child behavior therapy. *Behavior Therapy, 14*, 19-36.

Wahler, R. G., Hughey, J. B., & Gordon, J. S. (1981). Chronic patterns of mother-child coercion: Some differences between insular and non-insular families. *Analysis and Intervention in Developmental Disabilities, 1*, 145-156.

Wahler, R. G., Leske, G., & Rogers, E. S. (1979). The insular family: A deviance support system for oppositional children. In L. A. Hamerlynck (Ed.), *Behavioral systems for the developmentally disabled: In school and family environment* (pp. 150-177). New York: Brunner/Mazel.

Waring, E. M., & Patton, D. (1984). Marital intimacy and depression. *British Journal of Psychiatry, 145*, 641-644.

Warren, S. A. (1974). The distressed parent of the disabled child. In W. G. Klopfer & M. R. Reed (Eds.), *Problems in psychotherapy* (pp. 30-48). Washington, DC: Wiley (Hemisphere).

Watson, J. B., & Raynor, R. (1924). Conditioned emotional responses. *Journal of Experimental Psychology, 3*, 1-14.

Webster-Stratton, C. (1985). Predictors of outcome in parent training for conduct disordered children. *Behavior Therapy, 16*, 223-243.

Webster-Stratton, C. (1989). Systematic comparison of consumer satisfaction of three cost effective parent training programs for conduct problem children. *Behavior Therapy, 20*, 103-115.

Wells, K. C., & Egan, J. (1988). Social learning and systems family therapy for childhood oppositional disorder: Comparative treatment outcome. *Comprehensive Psychiatry, 29*, 138-146.

Wiener, N. (1948). Cybernetics. *Scientific American, 179*, 14-18.

Wilden, A. (1980). *System and structure.* London: Tavistock.

Williams, C. D. (1959). The elimination of tantrum behaviors by extinction procedures. *Journal of Abnormal and Social Psychology, 59*, 269-270.

World Health Organization. (1992). *Manual of the International Statistical Classification of Disease, Injuries, and Causes of Death.* Geneva: World Health Organization.

Zeanah, C. H., Keener, M. A., Stewart, L., & Anders, T. F. (1985). Prenatal perception of infant personality: A preliminary investigation. *Journal of the American Academy of Child Psychiatry, 24*, 204-210.

INDEX

ABOUT THE AUTHOR

Mark R. Dadds is Codirector of the Behaviour Research and Therapy Centre, Associate Professor of Psychology at the University of Queensland, Australia, and a well-known child and family therapist. He has published widely on child and family psychology including a previous book on family therapy with Matthew Sanders. In 1991 he received an Early Career Award for contributions to psychology from the Australian Psychological Society, Division of Scientific Affairs. Away from psychology, he is an active musician and restorer of colonial Australian houses.